TRUMAN SPEAKS

Harry S. Truman at Columbia University

Truman Speaks

COLUMBIA UNIVERSITY PRESS

NEW YORK

Second cloth and first paperback printing.

Photos by Richard Silverman

Copyright © 1960 Harry S. Truman

Published in Great Britain, India, and Pakistan
by the Oxford University Press
London, Bombay, and Karachi

Library of Congress Catalog Card Number: 60-8389
Manufactured in the United States of America

ISBN 0-231-02384-7 (Cloth)
ISBN 0-231-08339-4 (Paperbound)

CONTENTS

FOREWORD

Public lectures fulfill many diverse functions in a university community. Some bring to the campus visiting scholars of world-wide renown, thus complementing the intellectual fare provided by the faculty of the host institution. Others place before student audiences eminent leaders in various professions outside the academic realm, men whose careers exemplify Whitehead's dictum that "Education is the acquisition of the art of the utilization of knowledge." Both are important, even indispensable, to the life of a university. Both are perennially and deservedly popular.

It follows that a university welcomes the establishment of such lectureships in all great fields of human endeavor. For these reasons Columbia University was happy to accept the proposal, made in 1956, for the creation of the William Radner Lectures in the field of government and public service. Mr. Radner, a graduate of Columbia College and the Columbia Law School, had devoted his abundant talents to the service of our government. After his untimely death, his family generously established the lectureship as a memorial to Mr. Radner.

The University was understandably gratified when former President Harry S. Truman accepted its invitation to become the first Radner Lecturer. For this purpose, he was the guest of the University on April 27, 28, and 29, 1959. It was President Truman's wish that his talks be kept as informal as possible and that he be permitted to address himself primarily to the undergraduates. The result is the plainspoken and straightforward speech so characteristic of the President.

Mr. Truman spoke to the students on the federal government. His three lectures dealt respectively with the Presidency, the Constitution, and the menace of demagoguery to a democracy. In each case he spoke extemporaneously, and each lecture was followed by a panel discussion in which selected students of Columbia College were invited to participate. In addition, the President took part in a seminar for students in the fields of History and Government, and he also held what might be termed a press conference at a student reception.

In all these appearances the President encouraged students to ask questions freely and he answered all of them frankly. Tape recordings or stenographic notes were made at each session, and what is presented in this little book is essentially the transcript of each occasion as it developed. Thus, the record preserves the spontaneity and the lively "give and take" of a series of meetings from which the Columbia students derived pleasure and lasting benefit. Their distinguished guest lecturer was indefatigable, and so were they.

As the record indicates, President Truman's primary purpose was to impress upon his youthful audience the nature of their political heritage and their responsibility to preserve it for the future. He spoke to them out of a lifetime of political experience and out of a profound knowledge of American history. In a time when political apathy is uncomfortably prevalent among our people, his emphasis upon the duties of citizenship was a distinct service to the University community. I trust that this record of his days on Morningside Heights will be equally useful to the wider community of those who will read this book.

GRAYSON KIRK
President
Columbia University

New York City
January, 1960

INTRODUCTION

This series of lectures and discussions which were held at Columbia University on April 27, 28, and 29, 1959, was intended to give the young people who constitute the student body of that great University some idea of what they have in our form of government in this United States and what they must do to maintain it.

The basis and source of these talks are my thirty or forty years' experience in government, beginning at the precinct level and moving upward through the township and the county to the federal government.

To gain the proper idea of our governmental setup it is necessary to have as complete a knowledge as it is possible to obtain of the history of the evolution of government, from the old Greek city-states through the Roman republic, the Dutch republic, the French government after the Revolution of 1793, and the growth of the English government to its present form.

One of the most absorbing studies that can be made is that of the history of the Constitution of the United States, tracing the origin of its provisions and why these were incorporated in it.

I hope these informal talks given at Columbia—which are reproduced here in the same "off-the-cuff" style in which they were made—will stimulate the young people of our country to take a greater interest in the study of government and to gain the necessary knowledge in how to maintain a free government.

HARRY S. TRUMAN

Independence, Missouri
January 26, 1960

TRUMAN SPEAKS

Monday, April 27, 1959

ON THE PRESIDENCY

At 10 o'clock in the morning, Monday, April 27, 1959, the first lecture of the first series of William Radner Lectures was presented in McMillin Theater, Columbia University, 116th Street and Broadway, New York City. John G. Palfrey, Dean of Columbia College, presided. Grayson Kirk, President of the University, extended the University's welcome to President Truman. After President Truman spoke, Dean Palfrey moderated a discussion in which a panel of Columbia College students, the Dean, and President Kirk all exchanged ideas with President Truman.

Opening Remarks, by Dean Palfrey

Ladies and gentlemen, President Kirk will introduce our distinguished visitor.

Greetings, by President Kirk

One of the pleasant responsibilities of a university is to supervise and administer various series of lectures in the different fields of intellectual activity embraced by the university's offerings. As in other institutions, we have many such series, and over the years they have enabled us to bring to the campus some of the most distinguished men of the times in their respective fields. Seven years ago the University was made the recipient of a new lecture series endowment in the name of and to preserve the memory of one of our distinguished, younger graduates, whose death at the age of forty-three was untimely. He had been a graduate of Columbia College and of Columbia Law School. He had spent some time in the private practice of law, but most of it was spent in Washington, at the close of which period he was General Counsel to the War Shipping Administration. Before that he had been General Counsel to the Maritime Commission, and before that General Counsel to the Reconstruction Finance Corporation. After his untimely death, his family proposed to establish here a series of lectures to be given annually, or at least periodically, on subjects relating to citizenship and public service. Having very gladly accepted this proposal, obviously our first thought was the selection of the individual we should invite to inaugurate the William Radner Lectures. Our choice was not difficult to make, and very happily, we bring to you today, and for two succeeding days, one of the truly great men of our time. Disregarding all the myopia of partisanship, whether for or against this party, or this individual, or that, this man emerges, on the basis of a long record of public service, great courage, and a high degree of statesmanship, as a man whom we delight to honor as future historians will revere, President Truman (*applause*).

Lecture, by President Truman

Thank you very, very much. President Kirk, Dean Palfrey, and ladies and gentlemen, young and old, I don't see how anybody in the world can possibly make good after such a wonderful introduction by the President of this great University. I'm highly complimented and highly pleased, and I hope you'll be as happy when I get through with you as you were when I came in (*laughter*). It's always nice to have a grand reception, but it's much nicer to have a bunch of satisfied customers once you get through.

I consider it a very great honor to have been asked as the first speaker for this series of lectures. I was acquainted with the man for whom the lectures are named. He was one of the ablest of our public servants, and I think I am doubly honored to have been selected for the Radner Lectures on that account.

Now Missouri has had a number of notorious characters. The three, I guess, most notorious are Mark Twain, Jesse James, and me (*laughter*). Mark and Jesse are dead and I have to fill in for them (*laughter*), so here I am.

I want to talk to you about the Chief Executive of the greatest nation in the history of the world. I want to talk to you about that office not because it became, by luck, my duty to fulfill it once, but because I want you to understand it a little better than most people do.

The Presidency is the most peculiar office in the history of the world. There's never been one like it, there's never been one as powerful, and there's never been any head of government who has had as much responsibility as the President of the United States now has, and has to assume. You must bear that in mind in the talk I am about to give you on the subject. When I get through, I am going to go over there and sit down with these youngsters, and, if they want to ask me some impudent questions, I'll try to give them some impudent answers (*laughter and applause*).

When the President leaves his office, he is duty-bound to have a continuing and vigorous interest in the welfare of the country and the world. He has to do something, and there's very little that a man who has been President of the United States can do without exploiting that greatest of offices. You'll find in the history of the Presidency that there's never been a single man who filled that office who did not respect it when he left it. In no way did he use it in a manner of promotion.

Now I felt that I should, as far as I can, get the people who are coming on, and who are going to be responsible for the welfare of this great nation of ours, to understand, as nearly as I can make them do it, what they have and what they have to do to keep it. If I make some headway on that in these three days I'm here, I'll have fulfilled an ambition that I've had for a long time. I have found out that the people of this coming generation, this younger generation I call it—you people who are going to take over the affairs of this nation and of the world—are as interested in the welfare of the nation as I could possibly be; and you have to be pretty interested to be that way. And I want, as far as I can, to get you to understand just exactly what this situation is and what you have to do to keep it. You didn't get it for nothing. You didn't get it without blood, sweat, and tears, as Winston Churchill said. We had to whip ourselves for four years * before we decided that we wanted to have the kind of free government that we have. And for that reason, you've got to

* The Civil War.

4

get yourselves ready to maintain it. If I can make some contribution to that, I'll be very happy.

The President of the United States has six jobs. I'm going to discuss each one of them with you for a little while, and, as I said to you, you're going to have a chance to ask questions. If you can stump me, I'll be very happy, because then I'll have to go and do a little studying myself.

The first great job that the President of the United States has is set out in the Constitution of the United States. In the second article you'll find that he's the Chief Executive, with orders to take care that the laws are faithfully executed. The President is the representative of the whole nation and he's the only lobbyist that all the 160 million people in this country have. Now there are fifteen or twenty million people in this country who can maintain what they call lobbyists in Washington and other places around the country for their welfare and benefit, and it's a perfectly legitimate thing to do because it's the right of petition guaranteed in the first ten amendments to the Constitution. (Those amendments are the greatest part of the Constitution, in my opinion, as I'll explain to you later in another lecture.)

The very fact that he's the Chief Executive makes it necessary for the President to understand the nation, its relations with other nations, and its relation to the people here at home. If he does that, he's well on the way to accomplishing the purpose for which he was elected. He's got to understand people. In other words, he's got to be a good politician, and a politician is a man who understands government. I'm proud to be called a politician, for it's a great honor; when a good politician dies he becomes a statesman, and I want to be a

5

politician for a long time (*applause*). You'll find, with nearly all the great Presidents of the country, that they understood people and that they were good politicians.

Now as to the President's next job in the Constitution: he's Commander in Chief of the armed forces of the United States when they're in Federal service. He's the absolute commander of the armed forces of the United States in time of war. He's the commander of the armed forces when they're called out for any purpose, if he wants to take control of them. Nobody else can do it. It's his business to outline policy for the military and to approve policies which the military think he ought to approve. He has to know what the policies are about, and then he has to go to work on them. It's his privilege to appoint generals—and sometimes to fire them when it's necessary (*laughter and applause*). It's not a pleasant procedure at all. If you look through the history of the country, you'll find that James K. Polk had to do that; Abraham Lincoln had to do it four times, and one of the fellows—after Lincoln had fired him—ran against him for President. It didn't happen in my case (*laughter*).

The President is also the maker of foreign policy of the United States. The President is absolutely responsible for our relations with other countries. He appoints ambassadors, with the advice and consent of the Senate, to represent him in these other countries. The other countries send ambassadors to the United States, and the President has to receive them before they can operate. If he doesn't choose to receive one, the man goes back home, and relations with that country may be severed. The President directs the foreign policy of the United States all the time. No one else can do it. The

President has to do that. That's one of his jobs. As specified in the Constitution, he's the maker of foreign policy.

Then, he's one of the top legislators in the whole government. It's his business to inform the Congress, at least once a year, on the state of the Union, and to make such recommendations as he thinks are proper for the welfare of the country and for the peace of the world. He has to do that. That's called for in the Constitution. The President of the United States makes a lot of recommendations which he thinks are for the good of the country. Congress—made up of the Senate and the House of Representatives—usually tells him where to go—half the time. But he's still got to make the thing work. When Congress passes legislation, nobody can enforce that legislation but the President.

Those are his four principal jobs. He's got two more, one of which I was very much intrigued with. He's head of his political party. He sets the policy for the party that's responsible for the operation of the government; he must understand the workings of this approach to the operation of the government; and he must be sure that there is party responsibility for the policies which he makes. Whenever the time comes to elect a new President, the political campaigns are centered mainly on what's happened in the last administration on a national basis. I kind of like that. I was raised a politician and went from precinct to President. I know something about politics, and as I told you a little while ago, I'm proud to be in that position.

Here's another job that is just as interesting as it can be. You know, all the old dowagers in Washington are always pulling strings to get in on this one. As the head of the state, the President entertains all the visiting heads of state. He entertains kings and queens and princes and prime ministers. And usually, he gives a state dinner in honor of the visiting person. I've had state dinners for the President of France and the future Queen of England and the President of Mexico and the President of Brazil. Every time one of those great dinners comes up, you can only seat ninety-nine people in the State Dining Room in the White House, and you know what a time it is to get those ninety-nine places filled (*laughter*) without making some of the great old social leaders feel pretty bad because they're not on the list. But sometimes it does them good to be left off; they behave a little better after that (*laughter*).

Now there's been a great deal of conversation about the constitutional set-up, and it sometimes causes strained relations between the President and the Congress and the courts. Well, it was set up that way on purpose. It was set up so that no man-on-horseback could take charge, so that no man could become a dictator. The legislative branch of the government has control of the purse strings, and if you think a government can run without money, you ought to read the last budget (*laughter*)! It has the final say on how much money shall be authorized for expenditure in that budget. And that's one of the most powerful strings it has. It also has a tremendous number of other duties to perform. I want you to read that first article very carefully, and you'll see what makes the Congress tick, and why, sometimes, the President and the Congress have to clash. If they didn't, the government wouldn't remain free.

Then, there's another branch of the government known

as the courts, the judicial system. The Supreme Court is set up as the final say on whether laws are in conformity with the basis of the government, the Constitution. The Judges of the Supreme Court are great men, honorable men. We've had fourteen Chief Justices, and we've had about ninety-three Justices.

Now the records of that Court are in existence; and the records of the Congress are in existence; but the records of the Presidents have been scattered from one end of the country to the other and all around the world. I'm trying to remedy that. President Roosevelt and I have set an example on how presidential papers ought to be taken care of. I hope we can go through with it.

I don't know whether you know it or not, but the Chief Justice is not the Chief Justice of the Supreme Court. He's the Chief Justice of the United States. You read the law on that subject and you'll find that the Chief Justice has supervisory control over every court in the land—from the police court to the top court. He has to be an administrator. He has to know where he's going and what he's doing, and we've had some great Chief Justices. I'd venture to say that out of those fourteen Chief Justices there's hardly a high school youngster in these United States who can name four of them and why they were great. Some of them were great and some of them weren't. It's just like the Presidency. Some of the Presidents were great and some of them weren't. I can say that, because I wasn't one of the great Presidents, but I had a good time trying to be one, I can tell you that (*laughter*).

Well, in the operation of an emergency we need cooperation between the various branches. The President has to persuade the Congress to go along on things when an emergency strikes the country. He has to be sure that the procedure under which he is acting is constitutional and within lines that will be upheld by the Court. A great many things came about when I happened to be President of the United States that required decisions that were—some of them—rather unusual.

We transformed the policy of the country from isolationism into internationalism. If you don't think that was a job, you ought to try it sometime. I hope you'll never have to. But you would see exactly what has to be done to make this greatest republic in the history of the world run as a world leader. In order to do that, the President has to know how to get along with people. He also has to have a viewpoint that's national and international in scope. He has to understand exactly why he thinks he should go through with things that are done. Sometimes, there are plenty of people in the country who think he doesn't know straight-up from crossways, and I always got told about that when I was there. There were more people in the United States, especially newspaper editors, who knew more about running the government than I did. And I was there doing it (*laughter*)! I had a lot of fun, though, making them like it.

The Constitution provided an outline of the presidential office, but not a complete outline. A great many of the things for which a President is responsible have been brought about by custom and by strong Presidents. Probably in the question period, I'll tell you something about the Presidents who made the greatest contributions, in my opinion—but that'll be only my opinion—and you may not have the same opinion—I want you to study these things carefully.

Tomorrow I'm going to talk to you about the Constitution, from the standpoint not of a lawyer, but of a man who has legislated under the Constitution and who has operated the government of the United States as Chief Executive under the Constitution. I'm going to talk to you about it in practical terms. Maybe the lawyers won't understand it, but I think you will (*laughter*), and I hope when I get through that it will have made an impression on you, so that you begin to get interested in the greatest government that the sun has ever shone on. If you do that, my trip here will not have been in vain.

Now I thank you for your close attention to this dissertation on the Presidency, which is not complete, by any means. I'm going to answer some questions for you, if I can. If I can't, why then we'll go and look them up and I'll answer them tomorrow. We'll see just exactly how you can make the contribution that Almighty God intended you to make when you were born under our great Stars and Stripes. Thank you very much (*applause*).

Panel Discussion, Moderated by Dean Palfrey

Dean Palfrey: President Truman, my job is to moderate the panel discussion and I propose to get on with it; but I would like to delay it just long enough to add to what President Kirk has said—a word about Columbia College.

Every so often something electric happens at Columbia.

You can see it happen—most of you who have been around for a number of years. It happened this time. Columbia College is in a sense the host, because President Truman honored us by saying that he would like to talk to the undergraduates. He has honored us by wanting to come to talk to us and to be with us and by wanting us to talk back to him. And I think he will discover—I hope pleasurably—that Columbia College is pretty good at that (*laughter*). After ten months, from where I sit,* I think it is so. Unless the members of the panel are awed into silence, they will have some questions to ask and we'll get to it, but I wanted to say, President Truman, that the College welcomes you, the College salutes you. It's a proud occasion.

President Truman: Thank you.

Dean Palfrey: Now let me introduce quickly around the table the members of the panel today. On my right: David Thompkins; next, Robert Anderson; next, Riordan Roett. On my left: Robert Bird; next Raymond Lubitz; and finally Warren Weir. I'm tempted to get in my whacks before they do. Let me ask you about something that has occurred both in your administration and in the present one, namely the situation, looking at it from the point of view of the Presidency, when the other party controls the Congress.

President Truman: That's happened time after time in the history of this country. In 1946, you remember, I had that awful Eightieth Congress (*laughter*). It's not anything unusual, and it's good for the country, because there are times when things can be obtained where one side thinks he's doing the other fellow a little political damage, and the other fellow

* John G. Palfrey had become Dean of Columbia College, July 1, 1958.

may think he's doing the other side a little political damage, and what comes out is for the benefit of the country.

Dean Palfrey: It works?

President Truman: Our government works always.

Dean Palfrey: I'm not going to proceed in any kind of order from now on. I thought, though, that the president of the Freshman Class might have the first question.

Student: Mr. President, you spoke just a second ago about Congress being of the opposite party to the President. This seems to me that it might be a very strong point of conflict. I wonder if you could give me a brief idea how you can work with a Congress that is not of your party and somewhat opposed to your policies?

President Truman: Well, there are always leaders in the Congress, the same as there are in any other organization, and almost always those leaders are reasonable men. When the President has a real program and he wants to put it over very badly, why then he sends for those leaders and discusses the matter. He usually makes it bipartisan—he has his own party representatives there—and discusses what he has in mind. Usually he can work it out. Now that operation known as the Marshall Plan was put into effect in 1947, and the present Secretary of State,* who was influential with many members of Congress of his own party, helped to get the Marshall Plan over. The bipartisan effort then was the beginning of the long line of policy, foreign policy of the United States, which carried through as long as I was President. It has carried over, to some extent, now. Does that answer your question?

* John Foster Dulles.

Student: Yes.

Student: Mr. President, you said that during your administration the country moved from isolationism to internationalism. I would imagine that one of the ways you did this was by joining NATO and moving into Korea. Do you have any regrets about moving this nation quite so quickly into an organization like NATO? With the results that have been . . .

President Truman: I have not. NATO has been a very successful organization. It was one of the things that kept us out of a third world war.

Student: Do you really think it has been effective for us in working toward peace in Europe?

President Truman: There isn't any question about it (*laughter and applause*).

Student: I'm quite sure that it's easy to say that without any question it has been successful, but I wonder if it isn't more of a symbol of what the West would like it to be, rather than an actual fighting force of the future?

President Truman: May I make a suggestion to you? Go over there and talk to the commander of NATO, and you'll find out a lot that you don't know now, and it'll be good for you. What I want to say to you is this. Let me elaborate a little bit on it. (I didn't mean to be discourteous to you at all.) Here's the situation. In 1917 and '18, an effort was made to carry out the grand plan of King Henry IV, the greatest king that France ever had, and that plan was sabotaged by twelve men in the United States Senate. It was known as the League of Nations. Sabotaging of that plan brought on the Second World War. Between the two World Wars some of us spent our time trying to make the United

States realize that it had become a leader in the Free World and that it couldn't build a fence around itself, for the oceans were no longer walls to keep people away. They can get here now from Moscow in about three hours and a half. We can get over there just as quickly and maybe a little quicker. I hope we can (*laughter*). The thing that brought about the transfer of our country from an isolationist nation to an international leader is the very thing I'm talking to you about, and the man who was one of the greatest isolationists was named Vandenberg.* He was completely converted, as were half a dozen of the other isolationists, because they began to see the light. It was a gradual proposition. It's working, and it's going to continue to work. When it quits working, we'll be in the third world war. Just keep that in your mind (*applause*).

Student: Well, Sir, considering the evolution of the Presidency, under strong Presidents of the twentieth century, such as Theodore Roosevelt, Franklin Roosevelt, and yourself, do you feel that the historical concept of the balance of political power still holds true, in the same sense that it did when the Constitution was first written?

President Truman: There's no question about that. But don't start with the modern Presidents. Start with the ones that really implemented the government of the United States. There's an old gentleman by the name of George Washington who had more fights with Congress than any President since. (I couldn't say before because he was the first one—*laughter*.) He established the government as a going concern; then, Thomas Jefferson stretched the Constitution until it cracked,

---

* The late Senator Arthur H. Vandenberg of Michigan.

when he bought Louisiana—if he hadn't bought Louisiana, think what would have happened to us. There were France and Russia and Great Britain owning all the western part of this continent (Spain was also in on it but Napoleon finally took it away from Spain and we bought it from him), and the situation would have been terrific if Jefferson hadn't gone through with that purchase. The next man who came along and made a contribution over the heads of the leading Congressmen of the time was Andrew Jackson, who abolished the United States Bank and moved the financial capital of the government back to Washington. And think what Franklin Roosevelt did when he went in there. That's the situation that has developed all the way along. I could go on and name two or three more of these Presidents who have had just as much trouble and a terrible time with the Congress but accomplished what they set out to do. And we did it, when we turned this country from isolationism to internationalism.

Dean Palfrey: I don't think our panelist will let it go at that; he has another one.

Student: I just want to elaborate on that a moment. What I meant was that the concept was that the Congress would be an exact counterpoise to the Supreme Court and the President and a check to either of these, and yet, under Franklin Roosevelt the President almost assumed, well, came very close to assuming legislative powers.

President Truman: They had always done that. A President always does that.

Student: Well, power over the adjustment of tariffs, influence in foreign policy, in the actual shaping of legislation did increase under President Roosevelt, and President Har-

16

ding or President Coolidge did not do this—in other words, do you think that this has changed the system of counterpoise?

President Truman: Not at all.

Student: Not at all?

President Truman: Not at all. You ought to try to operate sometime with a Congress that doesn't like you. It's a lot of fun. You can get a lot of things done, if you know how to go about it. But there hasn't been any change in the counterpoise at all. The facts of the case are that the counterpoise has been emphasized by the strong Presidents, and it's been allowed to go to pot by those who weren't strong. I'll discuss that with you when you get around to it.

Student: We were discussing the relationship between the President and Congress. You say one of the functions of the President is to administer the laws. I'm sure many laws have, well, passed during your administration which you did not approve of, for example the Taft-Hartley Law. Do you think that it is the function of the President to administer these laws, to the best of his ability, even if he disagrees with them?

President Truman: Have you read the oath under which the President serves? Read it and see what an honorable man will do and what he should do. Of course if he doesn't like a law that is passed over his veto, and he leaves a record, the chickens usually come home to roost if he's right, as they have in several instances that I can name (*laughter*). But a President follows the constitutional set-up that makes him the Chief Executive of the nation, and whether he likes the law or not, he always tries to enforce it to the best of his ability. If he doesn't like it, and sees that it won't work, he

17

will go to the Congress and tell them why it won't work and get them to amend it. That's done all the time.

Student: But isn't there very often a great deal of leeway in the administration of a law where the President's judgment has to operate? When he administers the law, if a President dislikes a law, isn't it likely that he will not be as anxious to enforce it as if he did like it?

President Truman: Not if he's an honorable man. It doesn't make a particle of difference.

Dean Palfrey: One other point: sometimes I think that, as with the McCarran Act, very strict and very complete enforcement of the law was precisely that which identified its shortcomings and made its amendment quite a necessity.

President Truman: That's absolutely correct. It's the best way to get those laws amended and repealed (*laughter*). Enforce them thoroughly.

Dean Palfrey: Let me go back to this gentleman.

Student: Mr. President, having served as President and Vice President of this great nation, how much power do you think should be delegated to the Vice President?

President Truman: I don't think the power of the President can be delegated without tearing up the Constitution and having a legislative government, and I don't want that.

Student: What about delegation of other powers, such as being his personal representative in many things, as Mr. Nixon is?

President Truman: I think that's good judgment. I think that's all right. I had my Vice President at the Cabinet meetings—every single time it met. He and I discussed everything that was going on in the world. But you must remember that

18

he had been in Congress and had been Floor Leader of the Senate for many, many years, and he understood it very well. It's always the proper thing to have the Vice President in on what goes on. As Tom Marshall said, "There's only one heartbeat between him and the White House" (*laughter*).

Dean Palfrey: The concept of the role of the Vice President is one of keeping him informed just in case, or is it something larger than that, such as assisting the President?

President Truman: Well, of course, they're both in it, but the principal thing is to keep him informed so that when the responsibility is his, he'll know how to go forward with it. I can speak to you on that from experience. It's absolutely essential that the man who may be your successor should know exactly what's going on. It wasn't possible for me to do that at the time I was Vice President because we were in the midst of war. The President had to manage those things, although he delegated a great many things to me to carry out in the Congress. The Vice President's influence is much greater in the Congress than anywhere else, and he can be a tower of strength to the President in legislation.

Student: Mr. President, I wonder if you could elaborate on the point of what the President should do as the head of his party? Could you tell us some definite things that you think he should do?

President Truman: Why, certainly I can. He can get legislation passed that will help the people. He must be given credit for that because he can do it. He must be sure his party is functioning and accepting the responsibility for the operation of the government and that his people at home understand who is responsible. But the President himself, after he's been elected and sworn in as President of the United States, is the President of the whole country. He's not President of one party but he's the leader of one party, and party responsibility is what makes free government run. You can find that in any government that's free.

Student: Is it possible for the President to set the policy for his party when there's such a split as that like the Northern versus the Southern Democrats or the liberal versus the conservative Republicans? Or would you foresee, perhaps, any political party realignment of liberals versus conservatives, and see this as a better way for the government to function?

President Truman: All I can say to you is that's the way it's operated and I'm speaking from experience.

Student: Do you think this is ideal for it? Do you think this is the best way for it to run?

President Truman: Why, I can tell you that wherever there's controversy, things that are the best always come to the top. Now there's been a great deal of conversation about filibusters in the Senate. I've been through a number of filibusters—some humdingers, I want to tell you (*laughter*). Every time, all arguments that took place in those filibusters were an improvement for the information of the country at large. And when the various sections of a party have a falling out and discuss their differences, it's much easier to get a program that will work than it would have been if the discussion hadn't been carried on. If you get the country lined up so that the people who think in one way are all on one side and all the people who think the other way are on the other side, when you go to turn the government over for operation when the opposition gets in, you're going to have the same trouble that dictators have. That's the reason our government runs—because in both parties there are sections of every line of thought, and when the government is turned over to the other party, it continues to operate just the same as it did in the first place.

Student: Mr. President, it seems that your successor in the White House at the present time doesn't agree with you on that and finds it a better policy to raise himself above party politics and place himself on the plane of the statesman before he has passed the stage of a politician (*laughter*). I would seriously wonder if this might not be a better approach to the government of the United States—to rise above it all.

President Truman: How can you do that? If you're going to be the President of the United States you've got to be the President or not, and it takes a politician to be a President. That's no reflection on anybody (*laughter and applause*).

Student: Well it would seem that he finds it easier to assume the responsibilities of the American government, without assuming the liabilities of the party himself, to which he is supposed to belong.

President Truman: Well, your question has two answers and I wouldn't like to make them here (*laughter*).

Student: Mr. President, Mr. Eisenhower finds himself being the first President after that amendment that was lately passed. In other words, he can't run for a third term. Do you think this cuts down on the effect that he can have on the country and his job as President at the present time?

President Truman: Well, those Republicans and that Eightieth Congress just make a lame duck out of their President. And I think it's wrong.

Student: Do you think, however, that it has cut down, well, that he can't know his responsibility. What about his influence?

President Truman: Well, I don't think it's the proper thing, because, as I say, when Congress succeeded in getting that amendment passed (and I'll talk some more about that tomorrow), that tied the President's hands. I'm going to invite you to read the arguments in *The Federalist*—I started to say *The Spectator* * (*laughter*)—the arguments in *The Federalist* on that subject, you'll find that it's very carefully worked out. When the Constitution was adopted, those who were making that Constitution were young men. There were only a couple of old men in the convention; they were almost all young men and they were familiar with the history of government in the world. They knew what they were doing when they refused to handicap the President with one term. You take those states that have constitutional provisions to head off the governor from another term: they have an awful time getting through legislation for the welfare of the people. I know, because I live in one of those states.

Student: Mr. President, I'd like to go into the idea of the President as Commander in Chief of the armed forces. I cannot be certain about what I'm about to give you as a hypothetical situation, but I understand that in about 1945, as we were about to defeat Germany—rather were in Ger-

* The Columbia College student newspaper.

22

many—it was, I believe, General Patton who was roughly twenty miles from Berlin, about two weeks before the Russians took the city. The Russians eventually did take the city, and General Patton did not advance. Now I'm not certain that this is true. I can't verify it by any source or anything like that, but in a situation like this, what role does the President play?

President Truman: He takes charge of the situation. That's what had to be done. An agreement had been made at Teheran and at Yalta that certain lines would be drawn in Germany. It started in Quebec. I simply carried out the agreement, by ordering the troops to the lines which had been agreed upon. That's all there was to it.

Student: Mr. President, how dependent must a President of the United States be today upon his Chiefs of Staff? Given our present military situation, it would seem that he is merely official head of the armed forces of the country and that he must rely more upon his generals than upon his own judgment?

President Truman: Well, that's what they're there for. Those professional military men are supposed to know the military situation as it is in the world, and they're supposed to inform the President, so that he can make up his mind on what he ought to do in case of an emergency.

Student: I'm wondering if it wouldn't be better to pass the full authority over to the military men or to one military man?

President Truman: It would not! It would not! The first thing you'd have is a dictator and a man-on-horseback. The

President of the United States is elected by the people, and he's a civilian, and he ought to be head of the armed forces. That's what makes it safe.

Student: Well, perhaps an example would be the power given to General MacArthur in Japan in 1945 when he was made Supreme Commander.

President Truman: He got relieved when it was necessary (*laughter and applause*). And you'd never in the world have had him relieved if the Chiefs of the Staff had been in control of the policy of the country.

Student: Mr. President, you mentioned in your lecture that you would like to be given the opportunity to mention who were the greatest Presidents and why. I would like to hear this from you.

President Truman: Well, I'll have to do it hurriedly because time's running out, but I'll name the ones that I consider made the greatest contribution to the maintenance of the republic. Washington, of course, that's established; then Jefferson, who turned the government over to the people; and Jackson, who continued that policy; then James K. Polk, who expanded the country to the Pacific and gave us space as a continental power and a chance to grow into one of the greatest republics. James K. Polk paid the same price for that part of the country that Thomas Jefferson paid for Louisiana. Don't forget that. Then Abraham Lincoln, of course, who saved the Union; he kept the Union from breaking apart. There might have been four or five countries, just like in Central America if that war had been successful. (You know, my mother died unreconstructed; she never spoke respectfully of anybody who was on the other side.) Then, the next of the great ones was Grover Cleveland; he restored the Presidency to its proper place in the set-up of the government. He refused to be browbeaten by the Congress. And after Grover Cleveland came Theodore Roosevelt, who started the program of taking the government out of the hands of the great exploiters and putting it back into the hands of the people. Woodrow Wilson then came along in 1912 and followed through on that. If it hadn't been for World War One, he would have been very successful in obtaining what he set out to do in his first message. Then, when he finally worked on the peace treaty, he tried his level best to arrange world affairs so that we could not enter into another debacle like the First World War. He was not successful on account of those isolationists I was telling you about. They helped to bring on the Second World War. Then along came Franklin Roosevelt, who set the Presidency along the same lines as the ones I've named. He set the Presidency where it belonged and got the situation developed so that when the Second World War was over, we were able to establish the United Nations which, we hope, in the long run, will work. NATO and the Pacific treaty and operations of that kind that are perfectly within the frame of the Charter of the United Nations were also set up. And I want to say to you that the first decision I made when I became President of the United States—fifteen minutes after I was sworn in—was to go ahead with the meeting for the establishment of the United Nations. I was asked, categorically, if the meeting would go ahead, and I said, "It certainly will," and that's the reason we have the United Nations.

Dean Palfrey: Mr. President, what was the most complicated, the one single, most difficult decision you had to make?

President Truman: Korea. The reason for that was the fact that the policies of our allies and the members of the United Nations were at stake at the same time as ours. We were in the position where we had to enforce the situation; a great many of those friends of ours in the United Nations came in and helped. But that decision on Korea had to be made on the basis of world requirements; it was not entirely a decision of the United States, and every one of the allies approved it. So did the Congress, until they got it into politics.

Dean Palfrey: So far, we have had one silent member of this panel, but President Kirk may have something he wants to ask *(laughter)*.

President Kirk: I've been listening to this discussion, with a great deal of interest, and partly because it has revealed so clearly the inescapable role of the President as the leader of his party. I wonder, President Truman, if you would want to say a word more about what seems to be something very important, namely, the continued existence of a liberal and a conservative wing in each of our major parties? It seems to me this is a good thing, rather than, as was suggested here earlier by one of our student questioners, a harmful thing.

President Truman: I think it's one of the good things that makes this country great. You get all points of view in each party, and the leader has policies of his own. He sells those policies to the country. He's elected on that basis, and he can carry through those policies, but if this country were split straight down the middle, the first thing you know, we'd have a situation that would be intolerable. It would afford an opportunity to change the government into a legislative form of government. I never fell very much for legislative government. In 1946, when a Republican Congress was elected, there was a very highly educated Senator, an Oxford graduate, who made the statement that he thought I should appoint a Secretary of State (at that time the Secretary of Sate succeeded to the Presidency when there was no Vice President, and I had that changed after I got in there) who was in sympathy with Congress. Then, he wanted me to resign and said that if I got out the country could run much better than it would otherwise. Well, I said that I thought it would have been a good thing if this able Senator had been educated in a land-grant college in the United States, because then he'd know something about our government (*laughter and applause*).

Dean Palfrey: What do you think is the relationship between the President and the Secretary of State?

President Truman: The Secretary of State, the State Department itself, is the President's source of information on the feeling of every country in the world, and we get that through their ambassadors here and our ambassadors over there. The Secretary of State assembles all that information, discusses it with the President, and the President has to decide on policy and what the Secretary of State will do to carry that decision and policy out.

Dean Palfrey: Panelists, have you run dry? We're coming near the end.

Student: Well, Clinton Rossiter in *The American Presidency* writes, "It is up to the President, exercising his rightful power, to hold the lines of constitutional sanity against

27

those who would break through them in feckless quest of notoriety." He was referring to men like Senator McCarthy and Senator Jenner. Do you feel that you successfully held the lines of constitutional sanity against congressional hysteria?

President Truman: I'm going to lecture to you, day after tomorrow, on congressional hysteria and ordinary hysteria and hysteria as it happens anywhere in this United States, and I'll discuss that whole question with you then, if you'll allow me to do it.

Student: Actually, though, I was just wondering if you felt that you had successfully handled the McCarthy problem?

President Truman: Well, I want to tell you something. You historians will have to write that up yourselves. I can't tell exactly what the result of my administration was. I tried my best to make the necessary orders when it was necessary to make them. And what I want to say to you historians is that any Monday morning quarterback can win a ball game next Monday, but he can't do it on Saturday (*laughter*).

Dean Palfrey: One final one that I'd like to get in was the question of the development of the executive office of the President which, in recent years, has now become, in a sense, a new center of considerable importance.

President Truman: Well, the reason for that is we have become the leaders of the Free World and the greatest of the world's powers. That's what brought that about, and the Constitution fits that development just as well as it does anything else when it comes up. It's strictly constitutional— what's been done under that situation. The courts have upheld every act and the Congress has approved every act that's been necessary to maintain the leadership of this great country of ours in the Free World. That's all there is to it.

Dean Palfrey: I was thinking specifically in terms of its being quite natural that there would be distinguished assistants to the President specializing in foreign affairs, and that there would also be a Secretary of State, and the question is the relationship between the two.

President Truman: There isn't any such thing. The Secretary of State is the President's representative for foreign policy. There are laws governing that very thing, and when you begin to split up the responsibility on these things, you can't take it away from the President, no matter what you do. If you're going to have some fellow that the Secretary of State thinks is on the inside with the President, how in the world is he going to be the man that advises the President on foreign policy? The President has got to depend on the Secretary of State.

Dean Palfrey: Yes.

Student: Mr. President, do you think it would be good if executive agreements were given more power than they now have? Do you think this would aid the President or do you think it would be bad?

President Truman: Well, there's plenty of power if the President wants to use it. I've made many an executive agreement on which I knew I couldn't get two thirds in the Senate, and it worked (*laughter*).

Dean Palfrey: Anything further?

Student: One final one. You mentioned, President Truman, that the President was the lobbyist for all the people, and once again I would wonder if it is not true that he's the lobbyist for only that part of the people that voted for him in the last election, or in other words those of his own party, the party members?

President Truman: Well, there never was a President who got 160 million votes. I said he was a lobbyist for 160 million people.

Student: Even though part of those people voted against him?

President Truman: It doesn't make a particle of difference. After he becomes President, he's President of the whole United States, but he's still the leader of his party.

Student: And he has no obligations to his party?

President Truman: No! His obligations are to the country, and when he meets those obligations, there'll be more out of that 160 million that will vote for him the next time (*laughter*).

Dean Palfrey: I think the time has come for a very distinguished visitor to continue a visit tomorrow which, I hope, will be as pleasant as this morning has been, at least for us. With great gratitude, President Truman, we close (*applause*).

President Truman: Thank you. Thank you.

Tuesday, April 28, 1959

ON THE CONSTITUTION

On Tuesday morning, April 28, 1959, again at 10 o'clock in McMillin Theater, President Truman delivered the second Radner Lecture. Philip C. Jessup, Hamilton Fish Professor of International Law and Diplomacy at Columbia and Ambassador at Large in the Truman Administration, presided at this session, and moderated the discussion between another panel of students from the College and the President, after he had spoken. Averell Harriman, former Governor of New York State, was one of the guests at this session.

Opening Remarks, by Professor Jessup

Mr. President, we would like to consider today just a continuation of yesterday and tomorrow a continuation of today. If we don't interrupt you too much by making introductions, we'll hope you will get into the habit of coming every morning and that's what we would like. You don't need to be told that you're always welcome.

Ladies and gentlemen, President Truman is going to talk this morning about the Constitution. He has a very good constitution of his own, but the one he's going to talk about is the Constitution of the United States. President Truman (*applause*).

Thank you. Thank you. Dr. Jessup, the panel, my good friend Governor Harriman, and all the people here who are interested in the government of the United States, I'm going to try to discuss with you my viewpoint of the Constitution of the United States, which I think is the greatest document of government ever put together, and discuss its operation from my viewpoint as executive director of a county, as a United States Senator, and as the President of the United States. It's a viewpoint of a man who hasn't been through law school but who has enforced laws, both local and national, and who has helped make laws in the Senate of the United States. As I told you yesterday, the lawyers may not understand what I'm talking about, but all of you, I think, will be informed, so that if you became the President of the United States, you'd grasp the meaning of the Constitution. That's the objective (*laughter*).

The Constitution has a very tangible meaning for all those who work under it. You know, it took a long time to arrive at a form of government such as ours—centuries, in fact, before thinking men came to the conclusion that too much power centered in one place was the most dangerous form of government for the people who lived under it. Our ancestors, who were responsible for the construction of our Constitution, are among the world heroes in the establishment of government. I don't know whether you know it or not, but you're living under the oldest government in the world today. It's a continuing government—from 1789 until this time—and is now the oldest established government in the world. Now you study that a little bit, and I think you'll find out something that will be of interest to you. Governments in all the rest of the countries of the world have changed time and again in that period. Some of them have changed for the better and a good many of them for the worse. But our government remains what the Constitution made it.

The Declaration of Independence and the Constitution and the Bill of Rights are now assembled in one place for safekeeping and display. We venerate these documents, not because they are old, not because they're valuable historical pieces and relics, but because they still have meaning. It's about one hundred and sixty-eight years ago that the Bill of Rights was ratified (it was in 1792—now you do your own subtracting). But it's still pointing the way to greater freedom and to greater opportunities for human beings. It's a living document. That's what makes it so great. And so long as we govern the nation by the letter and by the spirit of the Bill of Rights, we can be sure that our nation will grow in strength and wisdom and freedom.

The Constitution didn't set up a government for efficiency. It set up a government that would operate in the interests of the people who live under it, and it also set up a government that would be in the control of the people who live under it, which is something that has not happened very often in times past. Sometimes in those republics about which you read, the Roman republic, the Dutch republic, and several others, when the people became tired and refused to support their government under whatever conditions arose, then they turned to government by one man. They turned to dictatorship as a way to get "efficiency." But we are guarded against efficiency of that sort. The Constitution guards us from dictators. It's pretty difficult for a fellow who is the President of the United States or the Speaker of the House of Representatives or the Chief Justice of the United States (and these are the three most important offices in the government of the United States) to come to the point where he can take over control of the government and tell you what to do and how to do it.

Everyone who holds office in the Federal government, or in the government of one of our states, takes an oath to support the Constitution of the United States. Now I've taken that oath so many times, I haven't got fingers and toes enough to count them—including the two times I took the special oath, the one that made the most impression on me and which I'm going to read to you. It's a very, very simple one, and it makes the chills run up and down your spine when you have to take it. Here's what the Constitution says:

Before he enter on the Execution of his Office, he shall take the following Oath or Affirmation: I do solemnly swear (or affirm) that I will faithfully execute the Office of President of the United States, and will to the best of my ability, preserve, protect and defend the Constitution of the United States. [So help me God.]

What could be more solemn than that? The Chief Justice of the United States administered that oath to me one evening about seven, or nine minutes after seven o'clock in the evening, and then I was the President of the United States. That was on the twelfth day of April, 1945, and there were only a few people present because it was such a sudden happening that not everyone could be notified. I even had a terrific time getting my own wife and daughter there to see the old man made the head of the greatest government in the history of the world. And it impressed me no end. I want to say to you that I still have the greatest respect, as I told you yesterday, for the Presidency of the United States and for the man who holds that office. I may not agree with him politically; I reserve the right to quarrel with him if I don't think he's doing the right thing for the welfare of the nation and the world. But my respect for the office and for the man is as great as it possibly can be, and I hope you—every one—will inform yourselves enough so that you can feel the same way toward the head of the greatest government in the world, of which you're a part. You're a part of it, just the same as though you were in Washington in a public office.

The presidential oath actually says to "protect"; that oath says to "protect and defend the Constitution." Every lawyer takes a similar oath when he's admitted to the bar, and when you become an officer in the United States Army and join the military services, you take a similar oath. There's only one oath for the President of the United States, but all the rest of the public officials, when they go into public office, have to take an oath, too. And right here, I'm going to say something that I will elaborate on tomorrow. I'm not impressed with this McCarthy idea of having students who have to have their education partly paid for by the government being forced to take a loyalty oath. They ought to learn what the government is about. But taking oaths won't teach them. Oaths are no substitute for teachers. I'll tell you something more about that tomorrow, because I think a test oath for students is silly (*applause*). Teachers who don't know enough to teach you about our great government have no business being teachers, and after you've learned all you can about it, if you become one who doesn't appreciate his government, you are welcome to go to Russia or somewhere else, and then you can satisfy yourself (*laughter*).

Public officials are another matter. The oath that our officials take has deep significance. Its simple words compress a lot of history and a lot of our philosophy of government into one small space. In many countries men swear to be loyal to the king, or to a nation, or to a flag, or to something else. We swear to uphold and defend a document, a document that sets up our living government. That's the reason why it is such a sacred document. Do you know, they're always pecking at it? There is hardly a single Congressman that at one time or another hasn't introduced an amendment to the Constitution. Well, you know, when you begin to legislate on the Constitution of the United States government, you're tinkering with something that will cause trouble forevermore if you succeed in getting it done. Why, a Congress or two ago there were 3,000 amendments introduced to the Constitution of the United States, and you know why they were introduced? Some bird wanted to go back home and say, "If I'd had my way, I'd have fixed this for you." He knew darned well he couldn't get it, but he put it in anyway, and the reason he did that was just simply to get a headline. Take that Bricker Amendment. It's one of the worst things that ever came up (*laughter and applause*). Well, Bricker got his reward in the last election. That's the way we handle things, you see (*laughter*). We didn't take him out and hang him, we just kicked him out of office, and that's a good way to do it. And that was in Ohio —I didn't have a thing to do with it (*laughter*).

The Constitution sets forth our idea of government, and beyond this, with the Declaration of Independence, it expresses our idea of man and his place in the world. Think of that now. It sets up the dignity of the individual and his rights. Do you know why that Bill of Rights has been attached to the Constitution and why it was insisted on by most of the great men who wrote that Constitution? It's for your protection against your government. And when the demagogues in Congress—or out—commence throwing bricks at the First Amendment and the Fifth Amendment and any others, they are treading on dangerous ground. They are treading on one of the protections that you have.

Now I've run congressional committees—two of them in fact. One was a subcommittee and one of them my own. And every single witness who came before my committee (the one that got the name of National Defense Committee) understood that when he appeared before that committee his rights were amply protected. And I never failed to get any information I wanted out of witnesses. They were perfectly willing to tell what they knew if they thought they were going to get a fair deal when they did it. I had more witnesses before the National Defense Committee than all the rest of the committees in Congress at that time put together, and the objective was to prevent scandals in the greatest war in history.

We spent $565 billion in that war, killing people, shooting away our substance, because we were trying to prevent this very Constitution from being overturned by dictators. That was what it was for, and it was right. But we had to try to do it without waste and mismanagement. My committee worked to prevent that sort of thing. I had nine Senators on that committee, four of them of the opposition party, and in the whole period of the operation of that committee, from 1941 until 1945 when I left the Senate, there was never a minority report.

The government officials used to use me as a whipping boy. I was talking to a fellow just yesterday who said he had been working on one of the great defense projects in Europe, and that when something would go wrong, his boss would come around and say, "You better look out. That so-and-so Truman will be on your tail in a minute," and the fellow would get the matter straightened out (*laughter*). I'm not bragging, I'm just telling you something (*laughter*).

In the 1860s they had a joint committee known as the Committee on the Conduct of the War and in Freeman's *Life of Lee*, you'll find that Lee made the statement that that committee was worth two divisions to him. They tried their best to make the committee that I had into a "committee on the conduct of the war," but I wouldn't do it. What I was trying to do was to help win the war, and I think we did make a contribution to it. It got to the point that the President would call me up sometimes and say, "I want to see you." I'd go down and talk to him, and he'd say, "So-and-so over here, I can't do anything with him, and he's causing me trouble. I wish you'd give him a poke or two." I'd do it and the thing would straighten out (*laughter*). That got me into a lot of trouble (*laughter*). He finally decided that maybe I'd make a good Vice President (*laughter*). If I'd gone along with the idea of a "committee on the conduct of the war," I'd still be in the Senate having a good time (*laughter*). I couldn't have a better time than I'm having here, though.

We believe that a man should be free, and our Constitution establishes a system under which men can be free. It set up a framework to protect and expand this freedom. The longer I live, the more I'm impressed by the significance of our simple official oath to uphold and defend the Constitution of the United States. Perhaps it takes a lifetime of experience to understand how much the Constitution means in our national life. Now I want to urge you, with everything I've got, to read that Constitution. Here it is. Here it is in this pamphlet right here. This pamphlet's got twenty-eight pages in it, and the pages are small and they're not half filled. You can read it in twenty minutes. You read it two or three times and you find something new every time you read it. You know, it took the Supreme Court one hundred and fifty years to find one word in that Constitution that appears twice, and that's the word "welfare." It took them one hundred and fifty years to find that out (*laughter and applause*). Here's what it says. I'm going to read it to you; then you can come across the word yourselves and maybe you can analyze it as well as the Supreme Court did.

We the People of the United States, in order to form a more perfect Union, establish Justice, insure domestic tranquillity, provide for the common defence, promote the general Welfare and secure the Blessings of Liberty to ourselves and our Posterity, do ordain and establish this Constitution for the United States of America.

Now I'll read you the point where "welfare" comes in again. It's in Section 8, Article I. You see, this Constitution is divided into articles and sections. It's as interesting as it can possibly be, if you'll just read it carefully. This Section 8 in Article I sets out that "the Congress shall . . . provide for the . . . general Welfare of the United States."

Well, we got into a whale of a lot of trouble before the Supreme Court saw that word. We found out that welfare was a most important part of the government of this great nation of ours, and that every citizen of the United States was entitled to the welfare that he had earned for himself under the greatest government in the history of the world. But it took us a long time to find out. You know, a lot of things that occurred during the history of this government were all right when they were said to be constitutional—for instance, child labor and long hours and small pay and all that kind of business. Those things were changed for the welfare of the people of the United States. We had to go through a lot of maneuvers, and we had to work on a lot of "a's" and "the's" and put in a lot of periods and commas and one thing and another, which the lawyers like to do, and we finally obtained a program for the welfare of all concerned.

In Jackson County, Missouri, when I was Presiding Judge, I was trying to build a system of roads and a lot of public buildings in the county. I called in some of the advisers to the court in the county and asked them if they would go along with me if I appointed the three leading lawyers in the county to draw up a program, a legal proposition, so that we could go through with county improvements. One of the lawyers who was a great fellow and a friend of mine said, "Judge, you don't want three lawyers to set that thing up. You'll have so many 'whereases' and 'therefores' you won't know what it means when you get through." Well, I drew it up myself and put it through. And in that state they had 783 laws and 300 of them were in conflict with the rest of them. And a fellow, in order to run the county, had to make up his mind about what he was going to do, and then send for the county counselor and say to him, "Find out whether this is legal or not. I'm going to do it anyhow." The counselor could always find a way to get it done when he had to, and then the judge who was running the county was on safe ground. If the judge went ahead and did it on his own hook, he might be indicted for something. They tried to indict me, but they didn't succeed (*laughter*).

The longer I live, the more I am impressed with the significance of our American Constitution. I want you to read it and think about it. It's a plan, but not a strait jacket, flexible and short. Read it one hundred times, and you'll always find something new. It confuses the layman, and I want to say to you that it's the best confusion for lawyers that was ever brought about. The lawyers haven't succeeded in doing anything to it but to make it work better.

I have nothing against lawyers. You have to have them (*laughter*). Whenever you're working under the common law and the civil law and all the other kinds of law that there are in the world, you must have somebody who has the time, the willingness, and the ability to put those things together and make them work under this document of government of ours, which sets out what shall and what shall not be done in the interests of the people.

One of the most interesting things about our government is the way the Constitution is divided; you'll find that it is divided into articles. The first article, as I told you yesterday, sets up the Congress. You ought to read all the provisions and the powers of the Congress. But the power in the Congress which means most is the power of the purse strings. They can say whether you can have money to do things, or they can say whether you can't have it. When you can't get it, then, that's all, because under our system you have to pay as you go. You don't go out and do things and say, "Come on, we'll confiscate your property to pay for this." It's one of the finest things in the world that only Congress can levy taxes and Congress has to appropriate before the government can spend. Then, the second article, as I told you yesterday, sets up the President, the executive officer, who carries on the government after the laws are made. And the third article sets up the courts and says how they shall be run. The Constitution itself provides that. Each one of these articles is to be enforced as the Congress and the law may direct. This helps to keep it a living document.

The Constitution hasn't been amended very often, and most of the amendments that we've had are valuable to the welfare of the country. But we've had some amendments that weren't so valuable to the welfare of the country—two that I know about particularly. One was the Prohibition Amendment. The demagogues got control of the country and thought that they could control the appetites of human beings. They found out that they couldn't do it and, instead, created the greatest set of rackets that the country has ever seen. We finally awoke to what they had done and then went back to common sense. I don't care much about whether a man drinks or whether he doesn't, but a government has no business trying to legislate on your personal habits. We finally found that out and repealed that amendment. Now the demagogues have saddled us with another one.

That wonderful Eightieth Congress I was telling you about yesterday (*laughter*) passed the Twenty-second Amendment, and I could do nothing about it. You see, the President doesn't sign the bills that call for new amendments. Two thirds of each House can pass an amendment and then it has to be ratified by three fourths of the states, and when it is ratified by three fourths of the states, it automatically becomes a law and a part of the Constitution. Well, a majority of members in the Eightieth Congress remembered that they didn't like Roosevelt very well, and they wanted to be sure that no other President of the United States ever was elected, as he was, in succession four different times, so they passed this amendment to the Constitution, setting out that no President could serve more than two terms.

They couldn't include me in it because I was the President, and I can be elected as often as I want to be. I'm going to run again when I'm ninety (*applause*). I've announced that a time or two, and you know, some damn fool looked the situation over and said, "When you're ninety, it's an off year," so I can't even run then. I didn't know I was going to stir up all that trouble (*laughter*). You see what I'm up against.

When they passed that Twenty-second Amendment to the Constitution of the United States, they made a lame duck out of the President who succeeded me—and he was their own man. It shouldn't have been done. You ought to read *The Federalist* that I was telling you about yesterday and the arguments that were made on the Presidency. You will find out exactly why the President was given a four-year term, why he was able to succeed himself as often as the country thought it needed him. Now a precedent was established by George Washington. When he left the White House —well, he didn't have any White House, he lived in Philadelphia; I got corrected on that the other day. When he went home (*laughter*) after he had been President, he had served two terms. After that, all the Presidents who could be elected for two terms—some of them couldn't—stopped at the two-term period. I think in most cases they couldn't have been elected the third time anyway, but a man did come along who could be elected to a third term, and under the conditions that were existing in that time it was necessary to have a continuing defense program. It was also the opinion of most of the people in the United States that the men who ran against him were not the proper ones to carry on that program. That's no reflection on anybody. Many of us have been licked many a time because the people thought that another man was better and it's good for us; it keeps us from getting a big head.

The Twenty-second Amendment is one of the worst that has been put into the Constitution, except for the Prohibition Amendment. I'm going down to the Senate at the end of this week and testify before the committee and tell them exactly what I think about that amendment. I've got a right to do it because it doesn't affect me. It wouldn't make any difference what happened to that amendment; if I wanted to run for President, I could. I can't say I could be elected, but I could run anyhow (*laughter*). I'm going to tell them that I think it ought to be repealed. The people who passed that amendment made a lame duck out of the very man that they might have elected another time, if the voters still hero-worshiped him as they did in the beginning. I don't know whether that's worn off or not—I hope it has (*laughter*).

One of the most important features of the Constitution is its provision for making laws. When a law is proposed, some Senator or Representative introduces a bill providing for certain things. The first thing that is done is that the constitutional lawyers, who work for the two Houses, look at it very carefully to be sure that it's in line with what the Constitution provides. Then, in whichever House it's introduced, it's sent to a committee, and that committee acts on it if it feels like it. It will hold hearings, find out what the thing provides for and what it will do to the rest of the laws that are on the books, find out whether it ought to be passed or whether it ought not to be passed. Then it's brought out and put on what they call the calendar. And, if you're lucky—I've had some bad luck with mine—and the term doesn't run out before the calendar comes to an end, why then you get a chance to present it to the House in which it was introduced, and then you try to get it passed.

I want to say to you that, I think, 11,000 bills were introduced in the last Congress. Eleven thousand, and hardly ever more than two or three hundred of them pass, and these usually are amendments to laws that are already on the books. You've heard these fellows who run for office say that when they get there, they're going to repeal half the laws, that there are too many laws on the books now. When they get there, they find that they can't do it, for the simple reason that there are too many other Congressmen with axes to grind.

Of course, sometimes you can get a bill passed by getting the chairman of a committee to make a deal with a chairman in the other House to put an amendment on one of his bills so that it will fit both Houses, and then sometimes you're lucky enough to get it passed by both. But there is another stumbling block; that bill then has to go down to the President of the United States. He can sign it, and he must do it within ten days. If he doesn't do it within ten days, it becomes a law anyway, unless the Congress has adjourned, in which case it doesn't become a law. But the President can also veto it within the same ten days. He looks it over, and if he doesn't like it, he sets out his reasons why he doesn't like it and sends it back to the House where it originated. Then both Houses have to pass it by a two-thirds vote.

I've found that that two-thirds vote is pretty hard to get in some instances. I sent a great many vetoes to the Congress—I think about one hundred and forty. They passed only a handful of bills over my veto. One of them was that horrible McCarran Immigration Act, which they later had to amend, and on which I helped to beat the opposition in 1948 when I was running for President. Then, there was the Taft-Hartley Act, which they're still monkeying with. As you know, if you read those hearings down there in the Senate, on the amendments to the Labor Act, you'll find that most of the conversation was about this so-called "Taft-Hartley Act." And do you know what they have been doing? They have been reading my veto message on the Taft-Hartley Act into the record, and that's just as satisfactory to me as it can possibly be (*laughter*) because I told them that the damn thing wasn't worth hell room, and they went and passed it over my veto. Maybe that's what made them do it. There were plenty of Congressmen and Senators who felt that I didn't know what I was doing, and didn't know how to do it. Maybe they were right, I don't know. Only history will tell that.

At any rate, I want you to understand that everything that's done by the Congress of the United States, by the state legislatures, by the governors, by the President, and by the courts is in conformity with that greatest document in the history of the world, the Constitution of the United States.

I hope I've instilled in you some curiosity about your gov ernment. That's what I'm here for. I'm no teacher. I noticed this morning, when somebody brought me a *Daily News*, that it says, "Professor Truman of the Electoral College of 1948" (*laughter and applause*). Well, if you gave me an examination to qualify as a professor, I'm afraid I would be sent to the foot of the class. But what I'm trying to tell you about is my experience as a member of the government of the United States from precinct to President, and to tell you of my respect for this greatest document of government and for the greatest office in the history of the world. If I can arouse enough curiosity in you, so that you'll look these things up yourselves, if you'll read that Constitution, you'll find out just what a wonderful document it is. It's a wonderful thing, you know, when you take a bunch of men—back in 1787—who got together in Philadelphia and worked on this thing all summer; and they had arguments over every single sentence that went into it. As the sentences were finally put together, there isn't a legal document in the world that is to be compared with the Constitution of the United States.

I want you to become familiar with it. I want you to understand what it means. It's a simple document. No matter how long it took the Supreme Court to find the word "welfare" in it, it's still one of the simplest documents there is in government. That's the reason it's so great and that's the reason it has lasted the way it has.

The way they tied it up so it can't be amended on the spur of the moment is another great thing. Whenever states begin to legislate their constitution, then they have an unworkable government. I know, because we had to write a new constitution in Missouri last year on that account. They had put so many amendments on it, nobody could tell what it meant. We don't want to do that to this other great document, and we won't, because everybody understands what it stands for.

Now, if you'll do me a favor, you'll read that Constitution, you'll study it, and then you'll read the history of the government as it has come along since George Washington. You'll find that it's been a workable, going concern for the welfare of the people who live under it. Now I particularly want you to read the best part of that Constitution—the first ten amendments. You'll find out why it is that you have absolute protection from being browbeaten in the courts, or anywhere else, when you're a witness. You can't testify against yourself. Do you know where that originated? It originated in Israel—in 700 B.C. In their legal approach, no man could testify against himself, and if he did, his testimony was thrown out. That's where that originated.

You know, there's an inscription on the Liberty Bell of

the United States in which it says, "Proclaim freedom to all the world." That was written in Leviticus, about 1700 B.C., or 1500 B.C., and shows you that this has been a growing thing, the liberty of the individual and his freedom to do what he pleases to do, as long as it doesn't injure anybody, under a free government of which he has control at the ballot box.

Consider those things. It's the greatest study in the history of the world. There's nothing that beats it. There's nothing that beats the study of government from the beginning and the why and wherefore of the greatest government of all, the government under which you live. Now, I hope I have instilled a little curiosity in you, so you'll inform yourselves on what you have. I told you yesterday what you have to do to keep it. You have to be alert, every minute, because if you aren't, there's always somebody waiting to take it away from you. We've had times when this country was in a terrible fix because they had passed laws and tried to enforce them against the Constitution of the United States. Now tomorrow I'm going to tell you something about the hysteria that brought those things about, and I'm going to tell you who the hysterics were and what caused them. I thank you a lot (*applause*).

Panel Discussion, Moderated by Professor Jessup

Professor Jessup: I'd like to make it clear that I'm presiding over the meeting and not over the President (*laughter*). Governor Harriman asked me, as we were coming in, whether I was going to moderate the meeting. That's an old-standing term, but that's not my intention. I hope the panelists will be courteous, but I hope they won't be too moderate. I am sure

that if President Truman would step out of character sometime and be just a teeny-weeny bit immoderate, that would
add to the interest (*laughter*). I'd like to introduce to you
the panelists here: starting at the end: Martin Kaplan, Simon
Weatherby, Dave Blicker; over here: Bob Fisher, Paul Na-
gano, and Dick Merrill.

The President has indicated very delicately something of
his feeling about legalistic interpretations of the Constitution.
Fortunately, Mr. President, none of the panelists are lawyers,
and the chairman isn't supposed to get into the fight (*laughter*). You didn't quote Walt Whitman, but I'm sure you like
that rhetorical question in one of his poems; you remember,
he says, "Why does the hearse horse snicker as it carts the
lawyer away?" (*laughter and applause*).

Well, gentlemen of the panel, it's up to you now.

Student: Mr. President, you mentioned the hindrance of
the two-term amendment to Presidents of the United States.
Now I wondered if you considered this amendment a hindrance
to all Presidents or just to possibly weak and politically inept
ones?

President Truman: No, it has nothing whatever to do with
personalities. I want you to read *The Federalist* and find out
why the President's powers were set up and why his terms
were not limited. That will tell you just exactly why if a man
can be elected, he should be. He's got to be elected before he
can exceed the two-term limit, and there have been very few
of them that wanted to be elected. Here's one. I didn't want
to be elected again. I'd had enough trouble the times I was
there, and you'll find that's the way most of them would feel.
But we were in an emergency, a tremendous emergency at that

time, and it was necessary to carry that emergency through by the people who were familiar with how to run it. No, there's no personality mixed up in this at all. I just think it's a bad amendment and I've always thought so. I was against it, but I couldn't do anything about it.

Student: Mr. President, in any consideration of the Constitution as a legal document, I suppose you would agree that it's important to consider defiance. What would you have done if you had been in the Presidency with the segregation issue when Orval Faubus tried to get around the Constitution's specific program?

President Truman: Well, I don't usually answer hypothetical questions like that, but I can tell you what could have been done. I won't say that I would have done it, if I'd have been the President (*laughter*), but the National Guard was called out, and it should have been called into Federal service and told to enforce the law and then they would have had to do it (*applause*).

Student: Mr. President, one of the most vital elements in the Constitution is the system of checks and balances imposed by the separation of powers. Would you say that sometimes this may tend toward a lack of coordination and inefficiency?

President Truman: Whenever you have an efficient government you have a dictatorship, and that's what we're against. Of course, sometimes it isn't as efficient as a dictatorship would be. Our check-and-balance government is set up for that very purpose—for your protection—so that those in charge can't tell you to go to jail or tell you to turn over everything you have without due process of law. The reason for its inefficiency is the division of powers. And there's noth-

51

ing like it in the world. Those gentlemen who wrote that Constitution knew exactly what they were doing. Your question is a good one, because if you want an efficient government, why then go someplace where they have a dictatorship and you'll get it (*laughter*).

Student: Mr. President, in 1952 the Supreme Court ruled you out of order in the steel seizure case; now I wonder how you think this decision will affect the actions of future Presidents, when they are faced with similar circumstances?

President Truman: My successor has been handicapped by it already. The situation developed in a peculiar manner. There had been necessary seizures all the way along the line. We were in the Korean affair and we were short of everything that was necessary to carry that on. We were supplying our allies with the arms necessary to go ahead. When the steel strike came along, it was the opinion of everybody that it would prolong that situation—which it did—but the steel fellows went to court, and I told them that if they could get the Supreme Court to say that it was not proper to go ahead and have the government run the mills, why then I'd abide by the opinion of the Court. Well, there were, I think, seven or eight opinions written on that thing by the Supreme Court, and not a single one of them agreed. There was a minority report by three of the Justices and the minority opinion was written by the Chief Justice. Eventually, the opinion of Chief Justice Vinson will become the law of the land. They've already had trouble because it is not.

Professor Jessup: Do you want to follow up on that?

Student: Yes. So then you feel that under the Constitution, as a living document, it would be very likely that this will change in the future—the rules of the Court will change?

President Truman: There is no question about that. They have reversed themselves a hundred times in their existence. It's a good thing they do. They find out they're wrong just like all the rest of us do.

Student: Mr. President, Charles Beard believed that the Constitution was drafted to protect the economic interests of the Founding Fathers. Do you accept this interpretation?

President Truman: No (*laughter*)! The Constitution was written to protect you and these people right here and it does it. Beard, you know, got a little childish in his old age and went off half-cocked (*laughter*) on half a dozen subjects.

Student: Mr. President, you say that the President—the person in the office of the President acts in conformity with the Constitution. But it's a very short document and, as you say, a flexible document. Have you, in the office of President, actually acted in conformity with it or just not in conflict with it?

President Truman: I've done both. Whenever the country is in an emergency and it's necessary to meet the emergency, nobody can meet it but the President of the United States. He never intentionally goes outside the Constitution. Sometimes he stretches it a little. You take Jefferson: when he purchased Louisiana, he stretched the Constitution until it cracked, but if he hadn't bought Louisiana, think where we'd have been.

Student: Then, Sir, you'd say the real virtue of the Constitution is not what it says, but what it does not say, that adds flexibility?

President Truman: The real strength of the Constitution, in a great many instances, is what it implies and not the words exactly as they are set down in the document. But if you transcribe that document and lay it down, you'll find that there has never been a President who has gone outside the provisions of that Constitution. Lincoln came as near it as anybody could because he suspended habeas corpus and did a lot of other things that he had to do to save the Union, but he saved the Union, and then the thing came back again into regular order. The same thing happened in the First World War and in the Second World War. The powers of the President in an emergency are usually authorized by the Constitution itself. Everything that was done by what they call implication is always authorized by law, either before or after the fact (*laughter*).

Student: Yesterday you spoke about executive agreements in foreign affairs, and you brought out the point that when you knew you couldn't get your two-thirds vote in the Senate, you would make an executive agreement and get around it. Now, an executive agreement has the same binding force as a treaty. . . .

President Truman: That's correct.

Student: So aren't you evading the Constitution, in a way, in making executive agreements?

President Truman: Not at all, because eventually we get those things into treaties, and then they're agreed to (*laughter*).

Student: Sir, if you take the position that there are ways in which you can circumvent the Constitution, aren't you going away from the fact that you pointed out that there's a fundamental law which everyone should agree with, everyone should conform to? Doesn't this indicate a sphere of political maneuvering which may be inimical eventually in its effects?

President Truman: No, no, I don't think so. I'll tell you the reason for executive agreements. In a great many instances, they were brought about by the emergency under which we were operating, during the ending of the Second World War and the Korean affair and the beginning of a return to a peacetime economy. Those executive agreements were made in the interests of preventing, in some instances, the other countries from going completely bankrupt and joining the Communists. I think it was worth while to try to keep them from doing it.

Student: Well, would you believe, for example, in the steel seizure case, that this may be a bad precedent, that this may be tinkering with the Constitution which no longer may be beneficial?

President Truman: No, I don't think so. I don't think that any President wants to tinker with the Constitution. I know I didn't. I just wanted to make it work, and I think I did.

Student: Well, this is a pretty broad area, saying that in an emergency the President can do certain things. Who's to determine what the emergency is and what the President can do?

President Truman: The President declares the emergency himself, and it has to be agreed to, in one way or another, by the Congress of the United States. That makes it a real emergency; you'll find that Congress usually passes the legal authorizations, or appropriations, or whatever else is needed for him to carry through with the thing and save the country. That's all there is to it. You read your history on that, and you'll find that every great President has had to do things of that sort. And Congress has backed him up.

Student: Don't you feel that there is a considerable amount of carry-over from the time of the emergency into peacetime? That powers that you assumed in an emergency tend to carry over to other times and are then in violation of the Constitution?

President Truman: No, I don't think that's true, because usually those powers are repealed immediately, as soon as it can possibly be done. Sometimes, while that's being done, events arise in which it becomes necessary to use some of those emergency powers, and that's what has been done. Of course, you'll find that the opposition and that terrible press with which I had to work always knew what I was doing wrong, and that I ought to be impeached, but it never happened.

Student: Doesn't the broad area of implied powers enable a partisan faction or a party in Congress to legislate the Constitution? Legislate the meanings and the interpretations of the Constitution to their own ends?

President Truman: Well, it's been tried, but it never worked, because the President has as much right to interpret the Constitution as the Congress does, and he usually vetoes that sort of a bill.

Student: Sir, if I could get back to the steel seizure business in 1952, for a moment: you seized the steel mills, citing, I believe, as your right, the broad power to execute a legislative program.

President Truman: That's right.

Student: Namely, the price stabilization plan, and the defense plan, or the Marshall Plan. At the same time, the steel mills and the unions have their own rights of private property and collective bargaining. Now where do you draw the line in a case like this?

President Truman: There was no intention, in any way, to injure their title and their right to their private property, but the welfare of the country and the salvation of the Free World were much more important than any steel company.

Student: Yes, but if I can pursue this for a moment. During the Second World War, I believe, the President had power to seize plants during a strike under the Selective Service Act, or whatever it was, I've never been quite sure . . .

President Truman: It was an act passed especially for that purpose.

Student: Oh! I see. And in the Taft-Hartley Act of 1946 there was an amendment brought up, whereby the President should have the power to seize a plant, if it was to be struck, and this amendment was defeated.

President Truman: That's right. I vetoed the bill, too.

Student: Yes. But wouldn't you say that the Congress was specifically striking down this power of the President?

President Truman: No, I never thought so. I think that when a President is responsible for the situation, he has to act in accordance with his oath of office. That time, it was the Korean situation that brought on this thing. We were faced with an emergency, either to knuckle down under the Communists or to meet them head on. My objective was to meet them head on, and I'm very sure that if it had been possible to put the matter up to the Congress in those terms, they would have endorsed exactly what I did. But it went to the courts. I agreed to go to the courts, and I abided by the decision that was made.

Student: Mr. President, yesterday you pointed out that the President is the lobbyist for the welfare, for the immediate welfare of the people. And I think we can interpret from what you've said today that you think that the Supreme Court and the Justices, in some long-range view, secure the welfare of the people. Could you ever see yourself referring to the Supreme Court and the Justices as "the nine old men" when there is conflict between what you want and what the Supreme Court says you can do?

President Truman: No, I have the greatest respect for the Supreme Court of the United States. Sometimes I used to get awful mad at them when they went crossways and didn't do what I thought was the right thing, but that's customary.

Student: And you feel, then, that President Roosevelt's plan to change the format of the Court would be incorrect and was not quite appropriate?

President Truman: No. I wouldn't say that at all *(laughter and applause)*. I'll explain the thing to you *(laughter)*. You know, the first President who did that was a man named Abraham Lincoln. He increased the size of the Court during the War Between the States. The Court is so far behind with its work, it would be a good thing if we had fifteen Justices instead of nine, divided them into three sections, and let them, all three, work at the same time. We'd get up to date then with the legislation that's pending before them. That was the objective. Of course they charged Roosevelt with "trying to pack the court" to suit himself. Well, that can't be done, because I've tried it. It won't work *(laughter and applause)*.

Student: Mr. President, then you feel that when President Roosevelt did try to change the format, he did it because he felt the Supreme Court had too much work to do and should increase the Justices?

President Truman: Yes, I think that was fundamentally the cause, but he was charged with "trying to pack it" to suit himself. And as I say to you, whenever you put a man on the Supreme Court, he ceases to be your friend, you can be sure of that (*laughter*).

Student: Mr. President, hasn't the flexibility of the Constitution enabled the Presidency to become all out of proportion to the intentions of the Founders in regard to the balance of power that they originally established?

President Truman: Oh, no, that isn't the case at all. If you read Article I of the Constitution of the United States, the powers of the Congress are specifically set out. If you read Article II, you'll find that the powers of the President are specifically set out. But it's always the policy of the Congress, particularly when they're against you, to take over the control of the Presidency and tell the President what to do. A good President doesn't let them do that. He makes them stand in their place. His resistance is usually effective and stands up, as you'll find it, if you carefully read the history of the United States. It has nothing whatever to do with anybody taking over the powers of the other branches of the government. I submitted to the Court when I didn't think they were right on that steel seizure business, as I thought I should do. Now, they're crying because it happened.

Student: Mr. President, I wonder if we might move from

our Constitution to the constitution of a greater body in dimension, the United Nations. I wonder if you could give us your opinions about the effectiveness, the effects of it.

President Truman: Well, I'll give you an analogy on that. The Constitution of the United States was adopted in 1787, and the Bill of Rights was accomplished a couple of years later. But what happened was that there were people in Massachusetts and in New England who tried to secede. The western part of Pennsylvania tried to secede and General Washington kept them in the Union as he did in the rebellion of Massachusetts. South Carolina decided that they were going to nullify the tariff bill of the United States, and old Andrew Jackson sent them word that if they didn't obey the law he'd come down there and hang every one of them. They knew he'd do it, and they obeyed the law. Well, the same thing happened in 1861. The Union was completely broken up at that time, and it is necessary to meet these things as they come along. Then, after we'd whipped ourselves—it took us four years to whip ourselves—we began to implement this Constitution of ours and make it work right straight through the later emergencies we've had to face.

Now the United Nations is a very young organization, and it's not made up of people (as were the original thirteen states) who all spoke the same language and who had been raised under practically the same laws. But, if we have the patience to go along with this thing over a period of time— I don't know how long it will take—we'll begin to respect the operation of the United Nations. As long as it doesn't get into the corner of one set of people and one set of theories,

60

not paying any attention to the other set, we'll make the United Nations and the World Court work, and we will then be settling things by international law instead of atomic bombs. And that's what we're working for.

In 1919 or 1920, when the League of Nations was put up to the Congress, if we had gone through with that, by this time we'd have had a working international organization, and, in my opinion, it would have prevented the Second World War. We have to come to the point where we can settle these things by common sense and by what's right. Now Colorado and Kansas had a lawsuit over the water in the Arkansas River. They didn't call out the National Guard and go to war with each other at all. The reason for that was they believed that, based on this Constitution of ours, the way to get justice was through the courts. That's what you've got to work for. The United Nations is a young organization. You can't expect it to start right off. Why, the republic of the United States had an awful time getting together, and making it work as it is today. You don't know how lucky you are to live in this day and age under the greatest republic in the history of the world. If we could get that United Nations into the minds of the people as a place where nations can get judgment without being imposed upon, and get people to abide by the judgments of the World Court, then we'll reach nearly a millennium and have peace from then on. That's the way it has to be.

Student: You've been speaking, Sir, about the laws of the courts, yet a moment ago you mentioned that you had tried to pack the Supreme Court. Then am I to assume that you

61

agree with your critics who said that your appointments to the Supreme Court were not based on judicial ability but were political appointments?

President Truman: No, that's entirely wrong. The men I appointed to the Court were the same kind of men that Abraham Lincoln, Grover Cleveland, and all the rest of them appointed when they had the chance. But when measures have come before that Court and on which measures I thought the welfare of the country was at stake, why all those fellows I appointed voted against me.

Student: Mr. President, you would like to increase the number in the Supreme Court?

President Truman: I think the Supreme Court needs an expansion on account of the terrific pile of work that's behind them. And I can say that because I've got no authority to appoint anybody to the Supreme Court. Anybody I'd recommend now would be turned down; you can be sure of that (*laughter*).

Student: Mr. President, do you think the failure to enforce the segregation decision of the Supreme Court, in all instances, has led to a decrease in the respect that Americans and people abroad have for the Constitution? Especially people abroad?

President Truman: No, I don't think so at all. Perhaps respect has decreased abroad but not at home. This so-called "segregation thing" is a matter of good will and common sense. There isn't any reason in the world why good will and common sense won't settle it. Now I'll tell you a concrete illustration. I live in the state of Missouri. In the central part of that state on both sides of the river all the way down, and on the southern side, several counties are just as unreconstructed as South Carolina. When the decision of the Court came down—and it ought to have been made sixty years ago —we had not one little bit of trouble. We called the people who were interested together: the superintendent of the Negro schools, the Baptist preacher of the colored Baptist church, and the Baptist preacher of the white church; we had the mayor of the town and the presiding judge of the county court sit down and discuss the matter. Nobody's found any fault with the manner in which it has worked because there was good will and common sense. And if it can be done there, it can be done anywhere.

Professor Jessup: Mr. President, I'm afraid that our time is up. I'm going to undertake to speak without hesitation for the audience and say that its verdict is that a system which produced you is a good system (*laughter and applause*).

President Truman: Again, I want to thank this most intelligent panel. Their questions were what I had hoped they'd ask me. I tried to answer them to the best of my ability, and I hope, if I didn't answer them to your satisfaction, that you'll go and try to prove me wrong somewhere (*laughter and applause*).

Panel Members: Thank you, Mr. President.

AT A SEMINAR ON STATECRAFT

A special seminar, consisting of selected History and Government students of Columbia College, convened in Room 616, Kent Hall, Columbia University, on Tuesday afternoon, April 28, 1959, at 3:15 o'clock. It ended at 4:15. As part of the program in American Government which he offered the undergraduates of Columbia College, President Truman conducted the seminar, aided by Lindsay Rogers, Burgess Professor of Public Law, and Henry F. Graff, Associate Professor of History.

Professor Rogers: This is a group consisting of members of a seminar in History at Columbia College and members of a seminar in Government at the College. They seem to have grouped themselves by subjects, people in Government down that way and people in History up this way; and Mr. Graff and I have tried them out on the kind of questions that they might want to pose to you, and we weren't thrilled. Mr. Graff and I are going to keep quiet, or at least try to keep quiet.

President Truman: I will tell you this. You are welcome to ask any question on any subject you want to, and if I can't answer it, I will tell you that. Anything I don't know, I will just say I don't. This is not a press conference. Go ahead.

Student: Mr. President, what changes do you think are

needed to put the Vice President in a better position to take over the Presidency if, as in your case, in the midst of a crisis something happened to the President?

President Truman: All the President has to do is to keep the Vice President informed; to keep him informed on what goes on. His business, as assistant to the President, is in the Senate. If he understands, and the Senate is in favor of his position, he can do a tremendous job for the President where it needs to be done most of the time, and keep him informed of what goes on in the Senate—as far as the President's policy is concerned. All the President has to do is invite him in. A constitutional change is not needed at all.

Student: Mr. President, do you think the Senate is a better place to come from in order to go to the Presidency, rather than from a gubernatorial position?

President Truman: There are two things in connection with that. One of the advantages of being in the Senate is the familiarity with legislation and the program of the Presidents who have come before—if a man has been in the Senate, that is one advantage. One of the advantages of being a governor is the executive part of his experience, of course, to interpret things in the state legislature, all very similar to the Congress of the United States. There are advantages in both. I couldn't very well say which is the most advantageous, because you would be sure to charge me with prejudice. I sat in the Senate ten years, and I also gained experience as a county executive at home.

Student: Mr. President, do you think a presidential aspirant would be hindered by a legal education?

President Truman: No, I don't think so, if he didn't let it go to his head. Most Presidents have been lawyers—a great many have—and the lawyer's education is a wonderful thing, if he doesn't get too much mixed up with it.

Student: Mr. President, do you feel if he does that he is liable to be out of touch with his constituency?

President Truman: Well, to some extent that would be the case, but the principal thing is that government is interpreted by language, not the language interpreted by the government.

Student: Mr. President, do you think that you were adequately informed as Vice President?

President Truman: About the situation as to the foreign policy I was not, but with the domestic situation, of course, I was familiar.

Student: Mr. President, do you think, because of the lack of information about foreign policy, you made any mistakes, Sir, just errors?

President Truman: That is for you to decide. I don't think I made any of tremendous importance, but nobody gets along without any mistakes.

Professor Graff: Mr. President, are there any decisions that you made while you were in the White House that you have regrets about, do you think, seeing them in retrospect?

President Truman: The great decisions, I think, in no way need to be changed. There are a lot of small things that might have been done better, but the bigger decisions are standing up. That is the best test you can go by. Nobody can make a final judgment as to whether a program of an administration has been right or wrong until the results of those decisions have been worked out, and that takes fifty years. I have not been out that long. No one is perfect, and if anybody in this room thinks he is, he ought to put on his wings right now.

Student: Mr. President, yesterday, I believe, you said your greatest decision was entering the Korean war. May I ask why you feel that was greater than dropping the atom bomb?

President Truman: The atom bomb was no "great decision." It was used in the war, and for your information, there were more people killed by fire bombs in Tokyo than dropping of the atom bombs accounted for. It was merely another powerful weapon in the arsenal of righteousness. The dropping of the bombs stopped the war, saved millions of lives. It is just the same as artillery on our side. Napoleon said that victory is always on the side of the artillery. It was a purely military decision to end the war.

The Korea decision, on the other hand, involved a world-wide policy on the part of the Free World. It included the whole Free World. That is why the decision had to be made by all the countries through the United Nations. That is the way it came about. That is the difference. The other was putting in big guns, artillery.

Student: Mr. President, I wonder what your opinion, impression, was of Stalin, if different than that of President Roosevelt?

President Truman: President Roosevelt thought the same as I. The only thing was that we found Stalin such a blooming liar. I liked him a lot. It was much easier to make an agreement with Stalin. But Churchill kept his agreements and Stalin did not. That is a good lesson. I think Churchill was not as affable as Stalin. Stalin was a very gracious host, and at the table, he would grasp what was going on as quickly as anybody I ever came in contact with; but he was always talking through his hat. He didn't mean what he said. It took six years to find out. Of the agreements he made with the United States, he broke fifty-two of them. Of course, you can't transact business with corporations or right here around this table unless you deal with an honest man. Roosevelt and I felt that we had to try, so that there would be peace. It turned out Russia didn't want peace.

Stalin gave a dinner for me. Now the Russians start a state dinner with toasts, and at the dinner for me there were fourteen or fifteen or twenty-eight bottles that everybody thought was Vodka. Stalin was drinking a lot. The dinner was in my honor. I was sitting to Stalin's right. Stalin was drinking from a glass that held about a thimbleful. He had a little glass, that big. I became curious about just what he was drinking, and I said, "I want to try your Vodka," and I poured some into my glass and do you know, it was French table wine.

Student: Mr. President, in his interview last year Ed Murrow asked what you consider the most significant contributions you made during your administration. You said, generally, those in foreign affairs. On the side of domestic policy, what do you think is the most significant contribution?

President Truman: The veto of the Taft-Hartley Act.

Student: Why?

President Truman: Because it was unconstitutional. They are now fighting over it. Of course, the McCarran Immigration Act was another one. It was vicious.

Student: Mr. President, you used the Taft-Hartley Act against strikes.

68

President Truman: It was the only thing on the books under which we could operate. What should have been in there was taken out. It is not good law; it never has been; and labor and management are beginning to find out. I wish you would read my veto message on that.

Student: Mr. President, when, in 1948, did you know you had the Republicans on the run?

President Truman: From the start. They did everything I expected them to. You know, on the night in Philadelphia when I accepted the nomination, they had gotten out a platform that was a humdinger; couldn't have been better for the Democrats. That night, on the platform, I told them, that on the twenty-sixth day of July, Turnip Day, I was going to call a special session of Congress and let them decide whether they wanted to do what they brought out in their platform. The damned fools didn't pass one measure. If they had, I would have been licked.

Student: Mr. President, in May of 1946, when the railroad unions threatened to strike, and you asked for the power to draft into the armed services any members of the unions who started to strike against the government . . .

President Truman: That is exactly right. We were at war when it happened. Go ahead (*laughter*).

Student: I can't go very far now. What I wanted to ask you was: Do you feel that this is in any way denying the privilege of labor?

President Truman: In a great emergency you deny the privileges that are necessary, to save the country. I could tell you a story about that. I thought they were going to tie up the country during a reconversion situation that was terrible. I called in the Attorney General. I said, "Put them in harness like the rest of the boys. See how they like it." Somebody in the Washington Union Station said to a railroad engineer, "What are you going to do about this?" and the answer was that the fellow was going to obey the President because he didn't want to sit on a bayonet.

Student: Mr. President, did the Truman Doctrine originate as a direct result of the situation in Greece in early 1947, or was it just accelerated by the fact that the British withdrew their aid in February?

President Truman: This is what happened. It shouldn't be called the "Truman Doctrine." All these things, the relief of Greece and Turkey, the economic program that saved the Western world from going to pot, were parts of the foreign policy of the United States, which included the Korean action and the stopping of Tito when he threatened Trieste. All those things were the foreign policy of the United States; and when the British said they could no longer support Greece and Turkey, I called in the leaders on both sides in the House and Senate and told them we had to save Greece and Turkey, or the Russians would do what Peter the Great started out to do in the first place: take the Black Sea Straits, and that we didn't want to happen. So they agreed that the proper thing for us to do was to take over the situation and save Greece and Turkey. But all these things fitted into a policy to save the Free World from domination by the Communists, and that is how it happened. That is what it meant.

Now I will tell you a story about Tito's threat to me. A short time after the Germans surrendered in Trieste, Tito announced that he was going to occupy the city. I called Eisenhower, and Marshall, and the Chief of Naval Operations, and I asked the Commanding General of the Armed Forces in Europe how long it would take to get three divisions to the Brenner Pass. He needed, he told me, a couple of days. I asked the Chief of Naval Operations how long it would take to bring the Mediterranean Fleet into the Adriatic. He said about three days. I said to Tito, "Come over, Tito, I'll meet you at the Brenner Pass in about three days," and he didn't come.

When Stalin refused to move out of Iran at the time agreed, I sent him word I would move the fleet as far as the Persian Gulf. He got out.

That was all part of the foreign policy to save the Free World.

Student: Mr. President, I wonder if there is one particular incident, a particular point, at which it became clear to you that the alliance wasn't going to last, that we were going to have conflict with Russia?

President Truman: I didn't feel that was the case until after the Potsdam Conference, when they immediately began breaking agreements with us regarding Germany and Poland and Rumania and Bulgaria. Then I began to feel we were up against something we had to meet. That is how it came about. I had hoped, as everybody else did, that they would keep their agreements, and that all those countries would be free. After they broke those agreements, I came to the conclusion we had to do the best we could.

Student: Mr. President, in all jobs of leadership, there is so much detail work and administrative work to bear you down, how do you put that aside, and have time to make great decisions?

President Truman: You don't. You have to know details before you make the decisions to be able to determine policies.

Student: Mr. President, I understand that for a while the President had to sign for every movement of the Marine band.

President Truman: Those details didn't affect me. I signed my name 167,400 times during the time I was in the White House. Once the things were decided on, for instance, commissions and things of that kind, that would have to be signed by me, all I had to do was sign them and carry on the business, and answer the phone, and talk to a fellow across the table, and all at the same time.

Student: Mr. President, what about people who wanted to see you, especially Congressmen and Senators? Did you turn them down?

President Truman: I have never turned them down. I saw every Congressman and Senator. I never turned them down. I had to turn down some of the outsiders, but people who had to transact business never were turned down. I saw, I couldn't tell you how many thousands of people while I was there. I always saw the people in the government, in the cabinet. They would call me up and say there was a piece of business that required a decision from me immediately, and they would be in. When a member of Congress called up, if I couldn't see him in thirty minutes, I would see him the next day. I had a regular schedule, but no person who had legitimate business with the President was ever turned down. I did all that daily work you are talking about between five in the morning and breakfast, and the time after dinner and eleven o'clock, when I usually went to sleep.

Student: Mr. President, would you be willing to explain to us what led you to believe that the first atomic bomb had failed to achieve peace with Japan and made it necessary to drop the second one?

President Truman: It was a military procedure, under which the armed forces decided that it would be necessary to destroy both towns, the manufacturing towns for raw materials which were being sent to the Japanese in China; and the objective was, as nearly as we possibly could determine, to shut off the supplies to the Japanese. We believed that only the Emperor could surrender. The great decision was made that the Emperor would not be disturbed, because unless the Emperor told the Japs to surrender, they would not do it. The Japanese in China were ready to fight. They are good fighters.

Student: The reason I asked this was that it seemed to me the second bomb came pretty soon after the first one, two or three days.

President Truman: That is right. We were destroying the centers, the factories that were making more munitions. Just a military maneuver, that is all.

All this uproar about what we did and what could have been stopped—should we take these wonderful Monday morning quarterbacks, the experts who are supposed to be right? They don't know what they are talking about. I was there. I did it. I would do it again.

Student: Mr. President, when was it made clear to the Japanese they would be allowed to retain the Emperor?

President Truman: The very first thing done after they made the proposition to the Swedes that they wanted to surrender. One of the questions was, would the Emperor be tried as a war criminal? The immediate answer from me was, "No. He will not. If you want the Emperor, you can keep him."

Student: Mr. President, what, in your opinion, would be better? Would it have been better to have made it clear in the Potsdam Declaration that the Japanese would be permitted to retain the Emperor?

President Truman: How could you do it? When we asked them to surrender at Potsdam, they gave us a very snotty answer. That is what I got. They didn't ask about the Emperor. I said, if they don't surrender, they would be completely, totally destroyed. They told me to go to hell, words to that effect.

Student: Mr. President, this morning, in the lecture, you spoke about the World Court. You said that in the future a time would come when the problems would be decided on legal grounds rather than resort to arms. Could I ask you whether you feel now that the United States should subscribe to the operative clause in the World Court Charter without reservation?

President Truman: That is a thing that can be worked out in negotiations. Minor details, don't let minor details stand in the way of preventing another war in the world. I tried to draw a parallel between the United States and the Colonies, and the Supreme Court and the World Court, and all these things: if each side is willing to make the thing work, it can be done, in spite of the details.

74

Student: Mr. President, I would like to ask this question, that you invited. Who do you think were the worst Presidents? You named the best Presidents yesterday morning.

President Truman: I don't want to do that. I will name those that I don't think did the job as it should have been done at the time.

The first, John Adams. Then, Madison. While he was one of the smartest Presidents of the time, as a leader in war, the War of 1812, he was a failure. The militia and everybody else deserted. The only battle he won was New Orleans, after the war was over. Monroe was famous for his arrangements with the British. Monroe was a good President, but I wouldn't say a great one.

Van Buren was a schemer. He was a maneuverer, as you can see in all organizations. You have them here, I guess. He wanted to maneuver things by playing both ends against the middle. In the long run, he turned out to be a pretty fair President, but on account of his maneuvering he failed at that time.

And of course, "Tippecanoe and Tyler Too" didn't have any platform of any kind. The campaign was run on demagoguery. That is one time when demagoguery paid off. The Whigs were sorry for it afterwards, because a military President, William H. Harrison, wasn't born in a log cabin at all. He was a very rich Virginian, and obtained a lot of land in the West as a result of the Battle of Tippecanoe. He was the oldest man ever elected to the Presidency—I think sixty-eight at the time of his election. Harrison's death was caused by riding in cold inclement weather. He caught a cold and died of pneumonia.

He was succeeded by John Tyler, who was a very peculiar person. He was a Senator from Virginia, and in Jackson's administration he didn't agree with Jackson on the Bank. He resigned because he wouldn't go along with Jackson's policy. He was nominated on this "Tippecanoe and Tyler Too" by the Whigs, who arranged things so they could win, and they did. The only thing Tyler did that was of any outstanding value was to make the people understand that he was President of the United States and not Acting President, and he set the precedent, because he was the first Vice President to succeed to the Presidency by the death of a President. Daniel Webster tried to make him "Acting President," but Tyler insisted on being President in his own right. Otherwise, I don't know of anything in particular he did of any great value to the maintenance of the Union of the United States.

Franklin Pierce was in the same class, and was a Democrat, who didn't ever have a program. He agreed with the South, the North, the West, and everything and everybody else. He was nominated and elected. He did one of the most terrible things that could be done. The two great contributions to the War Between the States were the repeal of the Missouri Compromise and the Kansas-Nebraska Bill. Franklin Pierce signed both the repeal of the Missouri Compromise and the Kansas-Nebraska Bill.

Buchanan, from Pennsylvania, an easygoing fellow, as Secretary of State under Polk, tried to run the government, but when he got to be President, he couldn't make a decision.

Then, after Lincoln, Andrew Johnson tried his best to carry out the Lincoln program. I want to say, if Lincoln had lived, he would have done no better than Johnson. As I told you yesterday, he knew when to die. Johnson did his level best to be a constitutional President, and he knew more about the Constitution than any man ever in the White House; a self educated man, a strong person; I guess next to George Washington, the most tolerant and enlightened man in the White House.

Then Johnson was followed by General Grant, who didn't know anything about administration. He was very fond of his close personal friends. But Grant was still a hero. Grant even came near being nominated in 1880. He got more votes than any other man at the convention, and after thirty-six ballots finally Hayes, who was President, got in touch with the convention and Garfield was nominated. Study your history.

Well, the convention nominated James Abram Garfield. He was nominated and elected President of the United States. Nobody knows what kind of policy he would have pursued, because he was shot in the back a very short time afterwards by a disgruntled seeker after office.

He was succeeded by Chester Arthur, who had sideburns. He took all the furniture in the White House, loaded it into nine vans, took it downtown, and sold it at auction, and then filled the House with Victorian furniture. When I had to rehabilitate the White House, that old furniture could not be obtained for love or money. I wanted to put back in the White House the old furniture that Jefferson, Monroe, John Adams, and John Quincy Adams had brought from Europe. That auction was one of the most outrageous things that ever happened to the White House. In the long run, Arthur didn't make a bad President; no outstanding or earth-shaking decisions, but outside of auctioning off the furniture in the White House he wasn't bad.

Then Benjamin Harrison came along and sat still.

If you subtract Fillmore, the man who succeeded Taylor, who was elected on account of his being a military man, Grant was about the worst.

McKinley was shot, another case. He was succeeded by a strong President, by Theodore Roosevelt. Theodore Roosevelt was succeeded by William Howard Taft, a fine man, but no executive, and he became Chief Justice of the United States. I had a very good friend, a Republican in Kansas City, who was a very strong supporter of Taft, and he was a lieutenant in the 129th. (I am not filibustering. If anyone of you wants to ask a question, go ahead.) My friend told Chief Justice Taft he had been for him. He said, "Old Taft said, from the bottom of his boots, 'Young man, you are a rare bird. Where were you when I needed you in Chicago?' " He had a sense of humor.

Of course, the programs after Woodrow Wilson, by Coolidge and Hoover, were not outstanding. President Hoover is my friend. I like him, and he did a wonderful job when I asked him to in dealing with the world food emergency, after the war, and when he served as chairman of the Hoover-Acheson Commission.

Then you have got to draw your own conclusions when you get close to the time in which you live. You can't very well assay a man until a good deal of time has passed. On deciding whether programs and policies have been effective, all you can come to is a judgment, and you need perspective. You can't tell yet about modern times—about this administration, or mine, or Franklin Roosevelt's—I am afraid I won't live long enough to find out what you think.

Of all these older Presidents, Grant puzzles me especially. It was said, "Mrs. Grant received on Thursday afternoons at the White House; the General received anything that was offered to him." You know, I can't understand why. He was, in the field, a great general, and finally wound up the difficulty between the North and the South. He made a wonderful agreement with Lee on the final surrender. I just hate to think about the sort of things happening that did happen in his administration. Of course, that is the story they told about him.

Professor Graff: Mr. President, if I might, I should like to turn from this discussion to some of the things in the background of Harry Truman himself. When, Sir, do you think you came to accept the principles that lay behind the Fair Deal and the New Deal? Was it your own experience as a boy; was it related perhaps to your service with Battery D; was it related perhaps to your experience in the haberdashery business; did it grow out of your work with Harry Hopkins in the early days of the depression? Can you tell us something about that?

President Truman: You see, my father and brother and I, after my experiences as a clerk, as a teller in a bank, ran a 600-acre farm belonging to the family. My father and brother operated that farm, and the farm situation got worse all the time. Then I became interested.

I was a member of the National Guard of Missouri, and in 1917, when the war came on, I was a lieutenant in Battery D, and at Camp Donophan I set up, as manager, what they called a canteen, a PX nowadays, and it paid $2,200 back and $15,000 in dividends in six months. When I came home, my partner in the canteen and I decided we would go into business. We went into the men's furnishings business. I furnished the money, he furnished the brains. We had a most successful time for about two years; then old man Mellon became Secretary of the Treasury. He ran after the farmers, and put the little boys out of business, and we went broke on that situation, and in the meantime I had become a member of a group that was very much interested in the political situation.

When the depression came along, I was the presiding officer of the Jackson County Court, and went through all the trouble of keeping people from starving to death and making all kinds of work. I even made a contribution to the Republicans to attract the Republican convention to Kansas City and got more tickets than the Republicans did.

And then I went on from there. When Roosevelt went in, Miss Perkins was Secretary of Labor, and they called me up one day and asked if I would take charge of employment, as Employment Director of the State of Missouri. I told her I would do it part-time. She said that would be all right. I was supposed to get a dollar a year. I never did get the dollar. With my experience on the farm, and the results of what Mellon did to the little boys, and the consolidation of the banks, the Panic of 1929, I felt that the administration from 1920 to 1928 was really the cause of that Panic of 1929. I was very much interested in trying to get that straightened out, because I had always been a member of the Democratic Party at home in Missouri, and I could see what went on. I was in complete agreement with the policy and platform of the convention of 1932 in Chicago, which nominated Roosevelt. When he announced his program, then of course I went crazy about him and stayed that way until he died. And that is the way it came about. It is a matter of experience and background. My mother operated that farm. If my mother knew my position on civil rights she would have "disinherited me." My mother died unreconstructed.

You have to use your own judgment in these things. You have to let your own conscience be your guide. My father used to say, that is all you can do. One comment was on a tombstone I saw in Arizona: "Here lies Jack Williams. He done his damnedest." What more can a man do? Do the best you can. Sometimes you come out successfully, sometimes you don't. You have to have luck and ability and be ready to meet the situation as it comes. All this happened to me. I never thought I would go to the United States Senate, but then I never thought I would go to the White House either. Luckily, I had studied the history of the White House. I knew all about the Presidents before I went to the White House.

Student: Mr. President, you were in the Senate quite a while?

President Truman: Ten years.

Student: Mr. President, you know how many ambitious men have been in the Senate, ambitious to become President. Over the entire history of our country, how come so few make it?

President Truman: There were not nearly as many in my ten-year membership of the Senate who were ambitious to become President of the United States at that time as there are now.

Professor Graff: Mr. President, in the 1920s when Franklin Roosevelt was urged to run for the Senate, he declined because, he said, "It is the graveyard of presidential hopes . . ."

President Truman: It always has been; let's hope it isn't this time.

Student: You talked about the role of Presidents and those of military leaders who have not made good Presidents.

President Truman: Professional military men.

Student: Mr. President, you classify yourself as nonprofessional?

President Truman: You have to know something to be a President. You have got to be a jack-of-all-trades and know something about all of them.

Student: Mr. President, previous to the 1948 election there was talk of having General Eisenhower as the Democratic nominee for President. I think at that time you spoke in favor of him, or in fact, endorsed him previously, in '46 and '47. Would you want to say anything on that?

President Truman: I will tell you what happened. It has been distorted and turned around every which way. He came to see me one time. I said, "Are you going to run for President?" He said, "No, I wouldn't do that." (He later wrote a letter telling why military men shouldn't be President, and it is the best analysis you ever saw.) And I said, "Well, if you were running for President, I wouldn't stand in your way." I didn't say I was for him, because I knew he didn't know what he was, Democrat or Republican; and he doesn't yet!

Student: Mr. President, I believe that your administration,

82

in 1946, attempted to support a liberal, pro-democratic government in Argentina, or a group aspiring to be such. Unfortunately, Perón's group came into power, and became the leader. The question is: Is there a way to support a liberal, pro-democratic government without intervening in domestic affairs?

President Truman: This is a very difficult thing to do. You know, whenever any foreign country interferes in local affairs in other countries, it is always the best political step for the local politicians to attack the foreign country—you remember, there used to be a mayor in Chicago, Bill Thompson. He was elected four times, running against King George. You see the analogy.

Student: Mr. President, do you feel that our form of democratic government is not necessarily applicable to people in other areas of the world who don't have the same political tradition?

President Truman: We were trying, and it still is the best approach, to get people interested in their own welfare and their own country. The education of people will always bring to the front the liberty of the individual. It always has, in the whole history of the world; it was taught way back in the time of the Judges in Israel and has been going on ever since. In China, you know, the old governments, under the philosophy of Confucius, were always working for the welfare of the individual; and that is what made the Chinese such a strong family country. That has been destroyed over there now, but if you let the education of the people take place, and at the same time try not to interfere in their own domestic affairs, eventually they will come to free government. The best example of that is Puerto Rico, which would have been in rebellion if we had not set them up as substantially as we have.

Student: Mr. President, in your memoirs you mentioned there was some anti-Semitism in the State Department.

President Truman: It is still there.

Student: Mr. President, is that in regard to policy in the Near East, or personnel in the administration?

President Truman: It has to do with the international policy, and in the Near East, and Syria and Iran.

You see, all sorts of people make up this world, and there are about 3 billion people in the world, and only about 900 million that are white. You have to get along with the rest of them or you will be overwhelmed. I don't believe in anti-anything. A man has to have a program; you have to be for something, otherwise you will never get anywhere.

Student: Mr. President, are you anti-Chicago *Tribune?*

President Truman: It is a destructive influence that I am against. If they had some progressive, recognizable policy . . .

Student: Mr. President, I wonder if you would mind discussing Sam Lubell's interpretation in *The Future of American Politics* of your administration. He characterized you as a man who bought time, according to his thesis. He feels you were presented in your administration with problems that were essentially insoluble, at least at the present time.

President Truman: He never had a chance to settle anything, but he tells somebody else how to do it.

Student: Mr. President, he is not even suggesting that. He suggested that you felt that if these problems were unsolved, eventually you could resolve everything to a stalemate and that time would work on your side.

President Truman: He doesn't know anything about what I think; he never got inside of my mind; he never even talked to me.

Student: Mr. President, that is what I wanted to check.

President Truman: You have a right to ask any questions you want. These fellows who project what ought to have been, and what might have been, so something would come out— he was never in the government.

Student: Mr. President, he felt that in these three areas, problems of the economic cycle, the cold war with Russia, and the civil war in the Democratic Party . . .

President Truman: We have no civil war in the Democratic Party. We will have it straightened out in '60. I am sure of that.

Professor Rogers: Thank you, Mr. President.

AT A STUDENT "PRESS CONFERENCE"

After the special History and Government seminar on Tuesday afternoon, April 28, 1959, President Truman was guest of honor at a reception given by the students of Columbia College in the John Jay Hall Lounge. There, accompanied by Richard E. Neustadt, Associate Professor of Government, he held a "press conference" with the undergraduates. The tape of the first question was blurred, so we pick up with President Truman in mid-course on two-party primaries.

President Truman: In California, you know, they had a cross-filing proposition. They never had a two-party government out there until recently. They finally had enough sense to repeal that law. They also had it in Minnesota. We need a strong two-party system in this country to keep things straight. The people who are in charge of the government nationally and in each state and county and city ought to be answerable to some outfit that competes with them for public office. There ought to be somebody to pick out the flaws so that they behave themselves as they go along. That's the reason for a two-party system.

Student: In my own situation, I didn't know which party I wanted to belong to, but they say the Democratic Party . . .

President Truman: You picked the right one (*laughter*).

Student: What do you think about Senator Proxmire's and Senator McNamara's criticism of Johnson? *

President Truman: Oh, I think it's a publicity stunt. That's all.

Student: What about the so-called "liberal mandate" the Democratic Party had in November?

President Truman: Who's going to decide what the mandate is? There are just as many liberal Democrats in the Congress as there are crackpots, and you've got to take into consideration that it takes common sense to make these things run. This is a publicity stunt in my opinion. That's just my opinion, and now you're entitled to yours.

Student: What do you think, Sir, of the Democratic revolt in New York City led by Eleanor Roosevelt and Senator Lehman?

President Truman: Well, I understand they've patched up all their differences and they're going to celebrate my birthday on the eighth day of May. They're going to kiss each other and make up.

Student: Mr. President, I know you mentioned in one of your talks the Taft-Hartley Act as one of the bills passed over your veto.

President Truman: That's right.

Student: What I'd like to know is about the present issues that have been brought up in revision of the Taft-Hartley Act. Did they meet with your approval?

President Truman: Some of them are good. I'm not familiar with all of them, but some of them are good. And some

* Senator Lyndon B. Johnson.

of them are the result of the reasons which I gave the Congress that the Taft-Hartley Act was not a good bill. If you'll read the veto message, you'll find that some of these things they've tried to do were suggested in that veto message. Of course, I haven't had a chance to go into this thing in detail. You've got to be present and know all the background of these things before you can give a really intelligent answer. But the Taft-Hartley Bill was no good and still is no good. I know that much.

Student: I was wondering if you felt that the Democrats in '60 will come up with a real foreign policy alternative to what the Republicans are now offering, whatever it is. For instance, do you think they'll make a stand on the Rapacki plan of "denuclearization"?

President Truman: I don't know what that plan is, but I know that when the Democrats get in power we'll have a foreign policy you can understand. All the foreign policy the Republicans have is what's left over from the administration which I left there. I don't like to brag like that, but it's true.

Student: It seems they haven't been making the best of it, either.

Student: In last year's New York senatorial campaign, Senator Keating claimed that you need a great deal of experience to become a United States Senator. How much do you think you really need?

President Truman: Well, it all depends. I didn't have any experience when I went there. I sat on the side and tried to learn how it went, and I got along very well. Of course, the more experience a man has in any job, probably the better off he is. And if he goes off half-cocked before he gets that experience, he usually gets in trouble.

Student: Do you think that there's anything the President can do to help enforce recent Supreme Court decisions about Southern Negro voting rights? You know, recently the Alabama Supreme Court has said it's not going to obey the Federal Supreme Court, some of their decisions, that is.

President Truman: Did you ever hear about the Nullification Act in South Carolina when a certain old President told them he'd come down and hang them all if they didn't obey the law? All right, that's your conclusion.

Student: Mr. President, who do you think the next President of the United States will be?

President Truman: He'll be a Democrat, but I can't tell you what his name will be *(laughter)*.

Professor Neustadt: I'm going to make a suggestion.

President Truman: Shoot.

Professor Neustadt: Why don't you gentlemen sit on the floor? Then everybody can see the President.

President Truman: They can do that. Now my hinges won't stand that, but the rest of you go ahead.

Student: Mr. President, you said the next Republican nominee for the Presidency . . .

President Truman: I hope it'll be Nixon *(laughter)*. He'll be easier to beat than anyone else. I'm afraid I've said that too often and they might keep him out.

Student: I hate to bring up a touchy situation, a problem, but I'd like to bring up NATO for a moment.

President Truman: Shoot! NATO's all right. It's not touchy with me *(laughter)*.

Student: I hope not. As I understand it, the main reason behind European support for NATO is that the European countries feel the hope that the United States will aid them in the event of any aggression upon them by an enemy. Now with the development of nuclear weapons, do you think that the United States would be willing to risk entering a third world war if a small European country in the NATO pact were to be involved in an act of aggression?

President Truman: If you can name one that's likely to be involved, well then, I can answer your question intelligently. The objective of NATO is to hold the Russians in check, and it has done that very thing. That's what it was organized for. That's the reason for its existence. There isn't anybody with any sense at all who wants a nuclear war, the Russians least of all. And that's what kept them quiet.

Student: During the last two years of your administration there were many attacks, of course, on the security program for personnel that you set up. I think you set up a very, very strict security program and I believe that since then Dean Acheson has had some regrets about the program. Perhaps it went a little too far?

President Truman: It was an experiment, and it was to be arranged as we went along at that time so that it would be fair and just to everybody. I don't know what they've done with it since I left. We were still working on it when I left the White House. I don't know how they've used it. It depends altogether on what the enforcement has been, and who's been responsible for any injustices that may have been done. There shouldn't be any injustice to anyone. Of course, under the circumstances at that time, when there was some chance of an infiltration, something had to be done. But it was an experiment, and I hope that it will work out all right eventually.

Student: Mr. President, do you think a particular danger facing this country, now, is widespread inflation, and if so, do you think there's anything we can do about it?

President Truman: Well, there isn't any reason at all for the country being allowed to go to inflation with all the brakes we have to put on.

Student: Mr. President, when the opposition party runs on an issue of bossism and then wins an election, don't you think that the person who is under that image should be replaced?

President Truman: Well, I don't know, I don't quite understand what you're driving at. Use names and facts.

Student: All right. Last November the Republican Party ran on—one of their main issues was that the New York Democratic Party was led by bossism and they referred to Mr. DeSapio as the main boss. Don't you think that since this image has been shown and the people seem to have accepted it, that they should replace Mr. DeSapio with somebody else?

President Truman: Well, now, you'll have to talk to the Democratic organization which has charge of that. And I want to tell you something: when a leader is in the Democratic Party he's a boss, when he's in the Republican Party he's nothing but a leader. But there's no difference in them (*laughter*).

Student: Mr. President, what do you think the probability is of getting a ban on nuclear tests at the Geneva conference?

President Truman: I don't know. I don't think there's any possible chance of doing what I tried to do to begin with, when we had absolute control of them, of nuclear weapons. We offered real disarmament with enforceable inspection and the Russians refused two hundred and sixty-seven times.

Student: What do you think our policy should be with Castro and the Latin Americans?

President Truman: We'll have to wait and see how things turn out. You can't jump at conclusions right now. Let's see if he intends to install free government in Cuba as we installed it in the Philippines. If he does, why, it's all right. If he doesn't, he's no more than any other dictator. I hope the boy intends to do what's right.

Student: We generally support dictators in our foreign policy.

President Truman: I beg your pardon?

Student: We generally support dictators in our foreign policy and . . .

President Truman: No!

Student: . . . does that help them in any way?

President Truman: I'm always against dictators anywhere, any place.

Student: How about Spain?

President Truman: Especially the Russians. Spain's worse than any of them. I never have been in favor of Franco. He's no good.

Student: I believe this morning that you were asked what your single toughest decision as President was, and you said it was to go into Korea.

President Truman: That's correct.

Student: How about the decision on dropping the atomic bomb?

President Truman: That was not any decision that you had to worry about. It was just the same as getting a bigger gun than the other fellow had to win a war and that's what it was used for. Nothing else but an artillery weapon.

Student: How much postwar planning was there on atomic energy?

President Truman: There was enough postwar planning to try and get world-wide control of the nuclear discovery, and the only reason that we didn't get it was that Russia, as I told you a while ago, refused two hundred and sixty-seven times by count, or maybe more than that, but I know there were that many while I was there. What was that question you asked me?

Student: I asked you about Spain. I said that during your administration you not only recognized Spain but . . .

President Truman: Spain had already been recognized at the time I became President of the United States. I never had any use for Franco. That's all that needs to be said. I never gave him any house. He wouldn't let a Baptist be buried in daylight (*laughter*). That's the truth. He had to be buried at night in plowed ground.

What is it, young man?

Student: Do you think we should recognize Red China?

President Truman: I don't like Red China. I don't like any of those birds, but you'll have to see how things come out and, eventually, we may have to recognize them. But I don't like to do it. If I were there I wouldn't like to do it. It may have to be done, though.

Student: How serious is the Berlin crisis?

President Truman: You'll have to ask the President. I don't know (*laughter*). I haven't got any intelligence service where I could tell you. I hope it's not as serious as the papers make out.

Student: What do you think our policy should be toward Nasser?

President Truman: We'll have to wait and see how he turns out. We've tried to favor him, and then he thought he wanted to play with the Communists, but he seems to have changed his mind. Let's see whether he means it or not.

Student: In regard to this morning's discussion of the seizure of the steel mills, how do you think this relates to the due process clause in the Constitution?

President Truman: It was an emergency that had to be met, and that's what was done under that emergency. It had nothing to do with due process or the taking of anybody's property. That was not intended at all. It was to keep the thing rolling to meet the emergency. Two of the Justices I was telling you about had each recommended that sort of procedure when they were Attorneys-General, but they voted against it as Justices.

Student: In regard to the African independence movements, do you think that the United States should take a stand? The Africans have been demanding that the United States come out for free determination and we've been sitting on the fence.

President Truman: We came out on that, I expect, when you were a very small boy, and it's still in effect. We all believe in free government . . .

Student: Do you think that any open action should be taken . . .

President Truman: . . . by the people.

Student: Do you think that there should be any open government action in Africa?

President Truman: Well, now, you'll have to ask the man who makes foreign policy—I can't make it—and that's the President of the United States. I think he'd answer you, if you'd ask him.

Student: President Truman, this morning you talked about the Constitution. The last couple of years there has been great abuse of the Fifth Amendment. Do you think any . . .

President Truman: I don't think there's been any abuse at all. Resorting to the Fifth Amendment is a perfectly proper way to keep these committees that have no rules for procedure from browbeating a citizen. There's nothing wrong with it at all. It hasn't been abused.

Student: Don't you think so?

President Truman: No.

Student: Not even by some?

President Truman: If the committees thought a witness had abused the Fifth Amendment, why didn't they go to court and have the fellow prosecuted? The court lives under the Fifth Amendment, and he'd have protection. He doesn't have any protection before a committee. You ought to go down there some time when they're against you and let them cross-question you and see how it feels.

Student: Mr. President, in your first speech on Monday, you mentioned some of the functions of a President. Two of them were: (1) leader of the nation and (2) leader of the party.

President Truman: That's right.

Student: I was wondering if you could tell us what issue presented the greatest conflict between these two functions in your administration?

President Truman: Never had any conflicts on it at all. I was President of the United States and tried to represent all of the people. And I was also the head of my party, and I wanted the party to have responsibility for what I did, and the party took it.

Student: Mr. President, you spoke optimistically this morning about the chances of the United Nations' succeeding. But can there be peace and international cooperation without trust and . . .

President Truman: No, there can't. When we have a bunch of crooks to deal with, and that's what we've got in the Russians, there is no trust.

Student: And yet you seem optimistic about . . .

President Truman: Why, of course. We've had plenty of crooks in this country, and we've overcome them (*laughter*).

Student: Mr. President, what of the attempt to change the filibuster rule at the beginning of this year?

President Truman: When I was in the Senate, I voted for an easing of that rule. Under certain conditions, I think it would be all right. We've tried for a long time to get it changed so it would eventually be necessary to vote on any question. And I think, eventually, the Senate will adopt a rule like that, but filibusters haven't been serious enough to hurt anything.

96

Student: Do you have any further political aspirations?

President Truman: My political aspiration, as I told you this morning, is to run for President when I'm ninety! But they say that's an off year and I can't do it (*laughter*).

Student: Do you think we should try to ease tension with the Russians? Are there any ways to insure peace with the Russians? I'm wondering especially, what are your ideas on cultural exchanges?

President Truman: Oh, yes, that's a great help. Those cultural exchanges are one of the nicest, best things we've ever done to get a better understanding among the rising generation, and I hope that eventually it will work out so that we can be at peace. The Russian people are just like everybody else. They're good people. They're hard-working people, and they want liberty just like we do.

Student: Mr. President, what was the rationale behind the firing of General MacArthur?

President Truman: Because he disobeyed orders. If he'd had a brigadier general under him, and if the brigadier general had done to him what he did to me, he'd have had the brigadier court-martialed! I didn't have him court-martialed. I should have, maybe (*laughter*).

Student: Would you like to see Germany reunified?

President Truman: I would like to see it reunified, and eventually it will be—in the long run. I don't know when.

Student: Do you think it will be safe?

President Truman: Oh, certainly. It will be safe. I think they've learned a lesson by being licked twice on the subject.

Student: I was in Canada recently and I noticed there was quite a bit of resentment on the part of the Canadians against the American influx of industry up there. What are your feelings on this?

President Truman: Well, I don't know what that situation is. The Canadians and ourselves have always been the greatest of friends, and there's no place in the world where there's a border as long as the Canadian border maintained without any guards, and that's going to continue; you needn't worry about that. There are some industrialists who probably think they can grab something by raising trouble between us.

Student: On this morning's lecture on the Constitution, it seems that the present tremendous problem with the Constitution is whether or not the first ten amendments should be included under the due process clause of the Fourteenth. Now, it seems that the Supreme Court has been vacillating terrifically on the case of the Fourth and Fifth—whether or not they should be included under due process. Do you think that the Supreme Court should definitely take an attitude to include, in every case, the first ten amendments under the due process clause?

President Truman: I think the proper inference is that the Supreme Court has to include the first ten amendments and all the rest of the Constitution, when they consider due process. If they don't, they're not doing their duty.

Student: What do you think about Russia's present progress in Siberia?

President Truman: I don't know anything about it, but they tell me that it is very good and that it is going ahead, and I hope it is, because that's a country that can stand tremendous development, just like our West did, way back yonder about a hundred years ago.

Student: Mr. President, would you care to give us an opinion on the success of Secretary of State Dulles?

President Truman: I don't think that personalities ought to enter into this thing. He was a good negotiator when he worked for Dean Acheson and had a boss to tell him what to do. Now his record as Secretary of State will have to be considered from a viewpoint of what happens in the future as a result of his actions as Secretary of State. I don't like to make a political comment on a man who is in the hospital.

Student: But what I was wondering was simply this: Monday morning, you mentioned in your lecture that it is the President who is the maker of foreign policy . . .

President Truman: Oh, yes, nobody can make a foreign policy but the President.

Student: But in line with this, the Secretary of State is certain to play a most important role in . . .

President Truman: He's the agent of the President in the making of foreign policy.

Student: Would you consider the Secretary of State to be the next position?

President Truman: In foreign policy, he's the President's right arm, and he should be.

Come on, boys, I'll take you in turn!

Student: Mr. President, the original responsibility for the present restrictions of American military personnel in Saudi Arabia has been placed at the doorstep of your administration. Do you accept that responsibility?

President Truman: I never heard of it.

Student: The restrictions or the . . .

President Truman: I never heard of the restrictions.

What is it, young man?

Student: As an elected official, do you feel that a Senator, for instance, should vote on his own moral decisions, or should he vote for what he believes his constituents want?

President Truman: He ought to vote on what he thinks right. It's representative government. And we have a representative government. So a man can get the facts and make up his mind on what he thinks is right. And that's the way he ought to vote. If he becomes a demagogue then he does what you suggest.

Student: Your own selection as Vice President in 1944 was a fortunate event for this country, but conventions tend to consider the vice presidential candidate as an afterthought.

President Truman: Well, maybe I was too, so there you are (*laughter*).

Student: There have been in the past some, perhaps unfortunate selections. Can you recommend any change in the manner of nominating the Vice President?

President Truman: No, I don't think there's any reason for making any change in that line. With the past experiences that we have it should be the business of the convention to nominate somebody for Vice President who can serve as President. That's the objective of the thing.

Professor Neustadt: May I interrupt here?

President Truman: Yes.

Professor Neustadt: I'm informed that you have to leave in a few minutes. May I ask for just one more question?

President Truman: Yes, go ahead. You pick him out.

Professor Neustadt: This fellow, I think.

Student: Mr. President, do you think that America has progressed in thirty-one years to the point where a member of a minority group can be elected to the highest office in the land?

President Truman: I don't know about that. We'll have to wait and consider it. It should be. We should be in a position where anybody who feels he'd like to be President can run for it if he wants to. People have to make up their minds on that. I can't give you an answer whether a member of a minority group can yet be elected. You'll have to study the matter. I hope the time will come when that will be the case. I don't think religion or color or anything of that kind ought to enter into it. If a man's got the qualifications and the ability, then he should have an equal chance.

Professor Neustadt: Thank you very much for spending this time with us, Mr. President.

Students: Thank you, Mr. President, thank you very much (*applause*).

Wednesday, April 29, 1959

ON HYSTERIA AND WITCH-HUNTING

The third Radner Lecture of the first series was delivered by President Truman at 10 o'clock, Wednesday morning, April 29, 1959, in McMillin Theater. This was the final offering in President Truman's program at the University. Lindsay Rogers, Burgess Professor of Public Law, presided, and moderated the discussion between student panelists of the College and the President which followed Mr. Truman's lecture. Dean John G. Palfrey of Columbia College closed the series.

Opening Remarks, by Professor Rogers

There comes a time when a lecturer is so well known and has made such a hit with audiences that instead of being introduced, he should be de-introduced. That, I propose to attempt. I shall read an imaginary item from a newspaper, which you will conclude was obviously Republican. The writer of the item was Herbert Lawrence Block, better known as the cartoonist "Herblock." This was the item:

The nation has been once more treated to the unedifying spectacle of a former President of the United States shooting his mouth off (*laughter*) in a rash, ill-timed remark, characterized by unbridled partisanship and profanity (*laughter*). When reporters accosted Mr. Truman on his morning stroll yesterday, they enquired what he thought about the weather. In his cockiest, shooting-from-the-hip manner, Mr. Truman told the astonished group, "Boys, I think it's going to rain like hell" (*laughter and applause*)! The Missouri politician could hardly be unaware of the fact that his intemperate statement ran directly counter to the official weather forecast (*laughter*) which was "clear and sunny." He was, in effect, casting aspersions upon the present administration (*laughter*) under which the Weather Bureau operates (*laughter*). His words were apparently calculated to spread gloom and doom among the thousands who planned picnics and to lessen public confidence in the judgment of the President, who was already on his way to the golf course (*laughter and applause*)! We can well imagine the glee with which the leaders of the Kremlin must view this latest attempt (*laughter*) to create division and to sow disunity. To be sure, we did have some fourteen inches of rain yesterday (*laughter*), but to belabor that coincidence would be to miss the essential point of the matter: Mr. Truman is not an authorized weather prognosticator and, in fact, he no longer holds any public office whatsoever!

But we are very happy that he is the first lecturer on the Radner Foundation (*laughter*).

Lecture, by President Truman

Well, I appreciate that left-handed introduction. It's one of the best I've ever had. I'd rather have left-handed ones than any other kind. I did have some experience with the Weather Bureau, all during my career as a public official. Back home, one time, we had a weatherman, by the name of Pat Connor, from my home town, or from a suburb of my home town—he lived in Kansas City (*laughter*)—and he made a daily forecast. He went over to Clay County to a picnic one day when he had prophesied rain. It was clear, and some of the people there told him that there was an old man there who always hit the weather. You know, Pat hunted him up and said, "How do you do that?" Well, he replied, "I just read what this fool Connor says, and I prophesy the other way, and it's usually right."

I've been with you now, this will be the third day. I have discussed with you two things in which I'm vitally interested, the Constitution and the Presidency. Today I'm going to talk to you a little bit about periods of hysteria that have hit this country and what those periods of hysteria usually do to the Constitution. It's an interesting situation. If you go into it very carefully, you'll find some things that will surprise you in this great republic of ours.

Before it was even in existence, way back in 1692, over at Salem, Massachusetts, there was a very serious period of hysteria on witchcraft. There was a preacher who had imported a couple of servants from the Virgin Islands to his home. One of them was known as a fortune teller. Well, the girls around town got interested in her fortune telling, and then they began to act as if they had been haunted by something. They charged people with being evil spirits and witches and things of that kind. When that was at its height, they called back another preacher who had gone to Maine and had been away from there for ten years. They called him back and hanged him as a witch. There were about twenty people executed—nineteen of them were hanged, and one of them was pressed to death. The point was finally reached, when it began to come too close to the top officials, that the people decided maybe there weren't quite so many witches as they'd thought, and witch-hunting came to an end of its own volition.

Well, two hundred and sixty-two years after that, in 1954, I think it was, Massachusetts passed a law pardoning all those people. Two hundred and sixty-two years after! The law said that none of them were guilty of anything and that it was too bad it happened. Now, that's a travesty on justice! It makes the Supreme Court look like a hurry-up operation. But it shows exactly what can happen when people get stirred up over something, especially something that they do not understand.

Fear is what lies behind these outbreaks. In Massachusetts the colonists were afraid of various things. They were worried about privateering and taxation and things of that kind, and they were ripe for just such an outburst of hysteria. It was an awful thing, but once in a while we get caught up with something of the kind.

About a hundred years after this witchcraft thing, we went through the hysteria associated with the Alien and Sedition Laws. Fear was the cause, again, only this time it was fear of social revolution. And, as before, there were demagogues around ready to exploit the fear. People became afraid that on account of the French Revolution something was going to happen over here. They were terribly put out with the French, and the Federalists, particularly, charged everybody they didn't like with having been connected with the French Revolution. It was just as dangerous for a man to be called a Jacobin in those times as it is to be called a Communist now. And the Federalists fanned people's fears for political reasons, to keep their party in office.

Two awful laws, the Alien and the Sedition Acts were passed and signed by the Federalist President, John Adams. The Sedition Law provided that anybody who made derogatory remarks against a public official could be fined and jailed, and a great many people were. There was one old man who was a kind of preacher, who used to go around the countryside talking to people on politics and religion and anything else that they were interested in. The Federalist authorities charged him under the Sedition Law, and they carried him, a perfectly harmless person, all the way across New York in chains, and finally brought him to trial, fined him $200, and put him in jail for a period. This caused so much interest and publicity that people became afraid that the Constitution was not being supported.

When Thomas Jefferson was elected, he pardoned all the people who had been convicted under the Alien and Sedition Laws, and he wrote a letter to Mrs. John Adams, because she reproached him for turning people out of jail who had jumped on John Adams, the President. Here's what Jefferson said to her in the letter:

I discharged every person under punishment or prosecution under the Sedition Law, because I considered and now consider that Law to be a nullity, as absolute and provable as though Congress had ordered us to fall down and worship a golden image, and that it was as much my duty to arrest its execution in every stage as it would have been to rescue from the fiery furnace those who should have been cast into it for refusing to worship the image. It was accordingly done in every instance without asking what the offenders had done, or against whom they had offended, but whether the pain they were suffering were inflicted under the pretended Sedition Law.

It was absolutely unconstitutional, and both the Alien and the Sedition Laws were finally repealed. There were no more prosecutions after Jefferson had taken care of the situation. That's one time when the President of the United States interpreted the Constitution of the United States contrary to what the courts had been doing. I give you that as an illustration of what the responsibility of a President is. It is his job to see that the document I talked to you about yesterday is supported as it ought to be for the benefit and welfare of the people for whom it was written. I want you to remember that and keep it in mind.

About thirty years later we went through another period of hysteria called the Anti-Masonic time. There was a fellow by the name of Morgan up here in New York who said he was going to denounce and write up everything that the Masons had as secrets. I've always wondered what in the world he could have found to denounce, for their main secrets are brotherly love, belief in God, and truth. If you want to find out the rest of them, you'll have to join (*laughter*). There wasn't a word of truth in Morgan's charges, but he and the demagogues got people so worked up that they closed and destroyed four hundred Masonic lodges in the whole United States. There was a fellow down in Baltimore, by the name of William Wirt, who ran on the Anti-Masonic ticket in 1832 because he hated Andrew Jackson. Andrew Jackson, you see, had been Grand Master in the Masons of Tennessee in 1821.

This old man, Wirt, actually got seven electoral votes. He didn't do any harm to Jackson, because Jackson was elected in '32 by a bigger majority than he was the first time. But that shows what can be done. It also shows that, as always, the hysteria was fed by men with political axes to grind.

The same kind of hysteria was roused against the Catholic Church. Americans tarred and feathered Catholic priests and burned Catholic churches. People were stampeded by demogogic charges that the Pope was going to come over here and run the country, if we let all the Catholics from Ireland in, as we had been doing. Just another piece of—well, I can't say the word—just another piece of foolishness; let's put it that way (*laughter*). It goes to show that these things come in cycles. Well, the organization that was responsible for these outrages burned up a monastery, a nunnery, in Massachusetts, and they burned three or four Catholic churches here in New York. The same thing happened in Virginia and in one or two other states. It was one of the most disgraceful things that ever happened. The people who belonged to that organization had a habit of saying, when somebody asked them if they were in it, "I know nothing." Well, they formed the Know-Nothing Party, and Wirt received his electoral votes from the Know-Nothing Party.

The Know-Nothing Party didn't last very long, but I'll digress here to say that when another new party was formed in 1856, around a fellow named John C. Frémont, it was made up of what was left of the Whigs and the Federalists and the Know-Nothings. It was called the Republican Party. They took the name from Thomas Jefferson, because they thought they'd get farther along politically. (You understand that I'm not making a political speech, I'm just recording history to you (*laughter*). Go and look up all these things if you want to.)

Well, after this anti-Catholic debacle Abraham Lincoln became President of the United States and saved the Union, saved the country from being cut up and torn to pieces. After that, there was an organization formed called the Ku Klux Klan. Those Klansmen covered the waterfront. They didn't like people of color, they didn't like Catholics, and they didn't like Jews. The Ku Klux Klan was in existence for quite a while after the War Between the States and murdered many, many a good man because they thought he didn't do just as he should. Direct action was what they followed through on —absolutely contrary to the government under which they lived. It was a terrible organization. It was revived along about 1921 or '22, when I first started to run for office, and I had the best fight with them you ever saw and whipped 'em to a standstill! I never thought anything of an outfit that had to work behind a sheet with a mask over their faces. In the early 1920s that Ku Klux proposition resulted in the election of a Ku Klux governor for the great state of Indiana. He was such a crooked bird that they had to send him to the penitentiary after he left office. That's the kind of men they were when they worked behind a sheet. When they got out in the open, the people caught up with them. I have no more use for them than I have for a fellow who'd try to shoot me—and somebody did once, and I commuted his sentence from hanging to life imprisonment because capital punishment was contrary to the laws of his home territory.

I want to bring home to you what can happen when some

demagogue starts playing on the fears of the people and stirring them up for his own welfare and aggrandizement. It's the most terrible thing in the world. And it's not just a matter of the distant past. We've had it very recently. We've just finished this period of McCarthyism, which was one of the worst that this country ever suffered (*applause*).

We are still going through a period where some of our witch-hunters in the United States Senate and the House of Representatives are charging people with things that do not exist, any more than those plots dreamed up by the anti-Masons and anti-Catholics and anti-Negroes and anti-Jews. I've said many a time that I think the Un-American Activities Committee in the House of Representatives was the most un-American thing in America (*applause*)!

We've still got some of those persecutors left. One of them hooked an amendment onto a bill to help students who couldn't afford to go through college, a rider telling those young men that they had to take an oath before they could go to school. Well, now, if they wanted to make it universal and make the rich boys take the oath as well as the poor ones, then I'd be for it. But it's not necessary to have a thing of that kind. The demagogues want to do the same thing to the teachers. Now if a teacher hasn't learned enough to appreciate his government as the greatest one in the history of the world and to support it, there's no use in giving him an oath to make him do it; if he hasn't got enough sense to learn it before he becomes a teacher, he oughtn't to be a teacher! That's all I've got to say.

The latest period of hysteria in this country is connected with the name of Senator McCarthy, one of the very few men in the history of the country who ever was formally censured by that great deliberative body, the Senate of the United States. Now if you want to get into history, McCarthy made it, but with a record that I wouldn't want. It's a terrible record.

I want you, every one of you, to consider the episodes that I've called to your attention and, if you're interested, to look them up. And I want you to remember that in your time you'll have a demagogue or two. I've been through half a dozen of them. We had one from Louisiana once who was one of the funniest fellows you ever saw. He was dangerous too. It's too bad it had to end the way it did. Somebody down there finally shot him (*laughter*). A thing like that shouldn't happen—but . . . lawlessness creates lawlessness, always.

When a Senator gets up and makes a demagogue out of himself and misrepresents the facts to the people, he's one of the most dangerous men that can be allowed to run loose in this country. There's not much way that you can prosecute him, because whatever a fellow says in the Senate is privileged; he can't be charged with it when he gets outside. Some of them take advantage of that. It makes some men feel great, you know, to get up on the floor and attack somebody. I was in the Senate one time and an attack was being made on an old general sitting up in the gallery, and when it came time to recess the Senate, the Senator concerned asked Bennett Clark and me to walk across the street with him. Bennett said, "What's the matter? You afraid that old General so-and-so will come down and bust you open?" "Well," he said, "he might" (*laughter*).

I don't care what your politics are, I don't care what you

112

believe politically, and I don't care what your religion is, as long as you live by it and act by it. But you must watch out for these people who make mountains out of something that doesn't exist—not even a molehill! You'll have the experience. I've had a lot of trouble with these birds, and the best way to handle them is to ridicule them. You know, there's no stuffed shirt that can stand ridicule. When you stick a pin in that stuffed shirt and let the wind out, he's through (*laughter*)! That's the best way to cure them. And it's the only way that it can be done, under some circumstances, for the simple reason that I don't believe in sedition laws. It's a man's liberty to say anything in the world, if he wants to, as long as it is not slander. Of course, he has to pay through the nose if he slanders a man (*applause*). I've been slandered many a time and didn't prosecute, because I didn't want to give them any more publicity, which would have happened if that had come about.

I hope—I sincerely hope—that you will keep your minds clear, that you'll become familiar with the history of governments in the world, with the history of great religions in the world. If a man lives by what he professes to believe, whether he's a Catholic, a Presbyterian, a Baptist, or a Jew, he'll make a good citizen, because there's a moral code which was given to us by the Almighty God himself. If you try to live by the code which you pretend to believe, you will never get into trouble, because the foundation of that code is, "Do unto others as you would have them do unto you." That's the best cure in the world for demagogues and for hysteria.

I want to warn you, though, that sometime or another you will have experience with demagogues and with hysteria, just as I have, and you have got to stand fast, because when those things take place, the demagogues try to find a goat on whom they can operate. If you're willing to be the goat, you can have a lot of fun, but you sometimes have to have a good many fights, which is the way we've won what we have.

As I told you yesterday, this government is not to be handed to you on a silver platter. It was gotten by fighting of the hardest kind. We had to spend four years of civil war, whipping ourselves, before we made up our minds that we had the best government in the world! Now we have it! What I'm trying to impress upon these youngsters, all of you, is that you must be prepared to maintain it. It's yours. It's your responsibility. I've tried to make my contribution and now I'm through—even if I do run for President when I'm ninety (*laughter*). If you don't look out for the welfare of this great government and this Constitution of ours, it can very easily be destroyed. Read the history of some of the great republics of the past, and you'll find out what happened to them when people became fat and easygoing and didn't look after the interests of the government. It's up to you, to do your duty as a citizen, and when you don't do it and things go wrong, you'll have nobody to blame but yourself.

Now, I hope you haven't been too badly bored by these three days that I've been with you. I've had the best time in the world, as you could see. I'm trying to give you something that I received by hard work. I'll make it as easy as possible for you, but you've got to do a little work yourself. You've got to go to the roots of these things I've been telling you about and get the facts straight in your head. When you

114

have them in your head nobody can take them away from you. Not even the brainwashers can do that, if you have the facts firmly in mind. Now it is up to you to take care of these things. I'm interested in the welfare of this great nation of ours and I'm interested in peace in the world. I've always tried to make a contribution to these two things. I think that the leading nation and government of the Free World should be maintained in that position right along, but it's up to you now to take charge. Old stiffs like me are through. It's time for the youngsters to come and take responsibility. And you've arrived at the age where you can make your contribution. I don't see any dumbbells here. You know what to do. Now go to work and do it (*applause*).

Panel Discussion, Moderated by Professor Rogers

Professor Rogers: We have six panelists who will ask some questions. From the left to the right, they are, Mr. Henry Abel, Mr. Erwin Glikes, Mr. Edwin Kaplan, Mr. Ira Jolles, Mr. William Bishin, and Mr. Robert Berlind. Alphabetically, I think Mr. Berlind comes first.*

Student: Mr. President, my first question has not so much to do with witchcraft as with hysteria itself. Does it not seem to you that the opposite problem also exists, which is apathy? On Monday you made the statement that you thought it was a good thing that extremes are kept within a given party and in this way there is no national divide on various issues. Don't you think that in this way the problems generally become

* Mr. Berlind did ask the first question, though of course alphabetically Mr. Abel was first.

ironed out within a party, and, as such, the public is never confronted with them and can never vote directly on them?

President Truman: No, I don't think so. I've never had any experience in that line, but I know that when the American people, as a people, understand the circumstances and the truth, the demagogues don't last very long in this country.

Student: My point was that . . . any of the things which happened could have become very large political issues in a given election. This generally doesn't happen because the parties don't take extremes.

President Truman: Well, the matter is solved by the legislative branch of the government, and its verdict becomes a political issue. It can become a political issue principally from the two things you mentioned.* In all probability, it will become a political issue in the next campaign. The more people know about what goes on, the wiser they are when they go to cast their votes. I am perfectly willing to take the chance of airing everything that affects the people and the government of the United States, a state, county, or city.

Student: Mr. President, you once stated that the security agencies of the government are well able to deal quietly and effectively with the Communists who sneak into the government without invoking Gestapo methods. Could you acquaint us briefly with some of these agencies to which you were referring and the relationship of the President to these agencies?

President Truman: Yes, two agencies and the Attorney General's office are in control of everything of that kind: the Secret Service in the Treasury and the FBI in the Justice

* The "two things" the student mentioned were lost to the tape.

Department. There are also United States Attorneys' offices, under the Attorney General, all over the United States. Then, Federal offices and the district attorneys of the country all are well equipped to see that the welfare of this country is well protected, and they do a very excellent job. They do take care of a great many things that you never hear of that could cause a tremendous amount of trouble. I think that answers your questions.

Student: Could you tell me specifically how much the President is informed about investigations that are going on? How much control does he have over those agencies?

President Truman: He can get any information he wants. All he has to do is call them and they have to give it to him. Nobody can keep information from the President when he wants it. I know (*laughter and applause*)!

Student: Mr. President, do you think the fact that Julius and Ethel Rosenberg got death sentences instead of life imprisonment was an example of national hysteria over the fact that the Russians had developed the atom bomb?

President Truman: I was not on the jury and I didn't preside in the court, so I can't answer your questions intelligently. They had a fair trial. The jury decided on what they should have and they got it. Now I don't know how you can go behind that. They're already dead (*laughter*).

Student: Mr. President, you've said many times that you had great faith in the American people. Today I think you've manifested that more than usual, because you said that—at least you seemed to imply—that all this hysteria seems to have been aroused by demagogues. And I wonder about this, because it seems to me the people take part in these hysterical

117

demonstrations. In what occurred with the Sedition Laws so many people took part in it; it was not only the Federalists; it was even people who had not made any party commitment.

President Truman: They were all tried in Federalist courts with Federalist judges.

Student: That's right, but again you see it was the Federalists and people who were against the French. Weren't they?

President Truman: Yes.

Student: They raised the specter of the French Jacobin, yet it was actually the Federalists. . .

President Truman: That's right.

Student: . . . who caused all this. This, of course, is . . .

President Truman: Oh, no. I don't think the Federalists caused it as a party. I think it was just a wave that went over the country. It was something to talk about and the demagogues picked it up and there you are.

Student: Don't you think that the people had some responsibility for what happened?

President Truman: Why of course they did. And I'm trying to get you boys right here, and you girls, to assume that responsibility. That's exactly what I'm talking to you for (*laughter and applause*).

Student: Mr. President, you spoke about people witch-hunting, people running around with axes during a time of hysteria. I wonder if you might say what you think is the right thing for the private citizen to do at a time when people are running around with axes? Should he stick his head off, out, I mean (*laughter*)?

President Truman: If he doesn't stick his head out, he's

liable to get it knocked off by some of the things that these demagogues stir up. The people have to take control of things at a time like this by voting the people out of office who got there through demagoguery.

Student: But very often a thing like this happens when there just isn't any voting possible. I mean between elections and things, and the private citizen either has to say something and take the risk, or not say anything. Now this, in a sense, ties up with the question of capital punishment. Thinking of a hypothetical situation, where someone really was to take the risk and say something almost treasonable during a period of hysteria, and then was punished for this—when the hysteria died down, that person would be dead. In a sense, I'm just asking for your opinion of capital punishment.

President Truman: Why, I've never really believed in capital punishment. I commuted the sentence of the fellow who was trying to shoot me to life imprisonment. That's the best example I can give you. But I know what you're trying to get at. You'll understand that when enough people know the actual facts behind one of these periods of hysteria they help to cure it. They take the responsibility and the risk. Good men always have to stick together for good government.

Professor Rogers: Do you think television helped to shorten the hysteria period of Senator McCarthy?

President Truman: I sure do. When they saw him on television they found out just exactly what he was. You better be careful when you get on that television too (*laughter*).

Student: Mr. President, it seems to me that one of the lessons of the periods of hysteria that have recurred is how very often very responsible people in high positions are willing to go along with the hysteria at the very beginning until public feeling rises against it. I think one example of that would be John Quincy Adams in the Anti-Masonic agitation in the 1830s, who seemed quite in agreement with the agitation of that time. I think another example would be the fact that so many people—almost the entire United States Senate —spoke out so very little against Senator McCarthy when the hysteria began in the '50s. It seems to me that this is what gives impetus to ordinary people to not say anything and not do anything. Is there any way in which legislators and people in high positions could be made to speak out themselves and show the first signs of courage?

President Truman: Well, that depends entirely on the men themselves. If a man has the necessary strong convictions, of course he ought to speak out, especially if he is in a position where he can be heard. I don't mean that a man ought to go down the street and be a crusader all by himself, but he's got to be associated with those people who believe as he does. You have made a very excellent point there—that these men have been encouraged by people who thought they could profit politically—half of them didn't believe a word of what was going on, but they saw a chance to garner a few votes. What I'm trying to impress upon you is that you ought not to be caught in that trap. You want to use your head when the time comes to see that the fellow who is working under false pretenses—and most demagogues have to—doesn't get your support and endorsement. And what you said fits right in with what I have been trying to get over here.

Student: Sir, when a leftover of the period of hysteria

exists, such as the loyalty oaths on the loans for students, what do you think institutions faced with something like this should do? What I should mention, for instance, is that Amherst, Goucher, Reed, and Williams colleges have declined the Federal aid for loans because of this oath. These schools, I suppose, have funds of their own, but they are, in a sense, taking a risk. Do you think that institutions should take this risk at a time like that?

President Truman: I think the institutions ought to fight it for all they're worth because it's wrong. And if enough of them fight it, that will kill the demagoguery that made it. I think they are going to take care of that Senator who introduced it at the next election (*applause*).

Student: Mr. President, do you think that the incriminations which have resulted from the loyalty investigations have made citizens more reluctant to work for government and thereby made it increasingly difficult for the United States to get competent scientists, ambassadors, and just civil service in general?

President Truman: I think that is absolutely true. It has almost ruined the morale of the civil service employees of the Federal government. They've done some awful things to some very great men. You had one of them on the platform here yesterday with me, Philip Jessup. He was misrepresented and lied about to beat the band, and he faced it and went through with it.

There's a college—I believe it's called Fiske College—that has fired a professor because he didn't want to testify to certain things that that committee was trying to get out of him with a corkscrew. He took the First Amendment so they fired

121

him. I think that's awful. I think all the rest of the professors in that college ought to quit and go somewhere else, and then let's see what they do. I don't have a bit of use for that kind of business. That's just as bad as the Communists.

We were talking a while ago about these fellows being "hanged" for treason.* If they had been in the Soviet Union under the same circumstances, a firing squad would have stood them up against the Kremlin walls and shot them without a trial. We don't do things that way, and we shouldn't do things that way. Every man ought to have his day in court and should have the right to defend himself.

But when you commence picking on educational institutions, in the manner in which it has been going on here lately, as you say, it's just a leftover from this period of hysteria through which we went. And I hope the colleges—every college in the country—whether they're interested in the thing financially or not—will fight it for all it's worth, and then they can lick it (*applause*).

Student: Mr. President, there have been other types of hysteria besides the particular ones of which you have spoken. During the Second World War there was a great fear of Japanese infiltration on the West Coast and a policy of relocation was adopted. Now I wonder if you think this was a legitimate way of dealing with the Japanese citizens on the West Coast?

President Truman: No, I don't. I think that was a blot on our character as a free nation. Even though we were in an emergency, I was absolutely against it (*applause*).

* Julius and Ethel Rosenberg.

Student: Mr. President, would you tell us exactly what you felt about the Alger Hiss case when it was in progress and what you now feel in retrospect?

President Truman: Well, the Hiss case has been used politically for a long, long time, particularly where I'm concerned. I never thought much about the way they handled that Hiss case; in fact, I never thought he was guilty until he was convicted of perjury.

Student: Sir, one of the McCarthy battlecries for investigations was that Communists in the State Department resulted in the loss of China. Discounting this as demagoguery, and looking back as a—what you call a "Monday morning quarterback"—can you see anything that could have been done to save China from the Communists?

President Truman: No. The Communists in the United States had nothing to do with the downfall of China. What caused the downfall of China was that the government armies we tried to help in China surrendered to the Communists all the arms, ammunition, and money that we sent over there for their benefit, and those arms and ammunition were used to run the Nationalists out. That's all there was to it. There was so much what you call "baksheesh" in that government that you could not very well help it. That's what caused the trouble, not Communists in the State Department. There were no Communists in the State Department. That was a bunch of hooey and it never was proved. McCarthy started out with 105, and then got down to 80, then down to 30, then down to 12, and then didn't find any (*applause*).

Student: Mr. President, in 1952–54, McCarthy was at the

height of his power. Do you think the President should have intervened instead of waiting for Senate censure in the interests of the people?

President Truman: I think Senate censure was the best thing that happened in the whole business. The President could have intervened if he had felt like it, but I think the way it was worked out was in the best interests of the country. It gave the people a shining example of what happens to a man like that, and we didn't have to prosecute him, or do anything else to him.

Student: One of the great fears of a country caught by hysteria is that the police suddenly take on arbitrary power. Now recently there has been a great deal of attack on the FBI and its methods. How do you feel about these attacks?

President Truman: Well, some of them are justified. You give any organization police power, and it has to be watched all the time. You have to have the brakes on them just like you do on anything else, and when the police power is debauched by any organization—I don't care in how small a manner—they ought to be overhauled and the fellows get the punishment that they ought to have.

Student: What do you think of J. Edgar Hoover?

President Truman: Why, I like J. Edgar Hoover. He was as loyal to me as a man can be while I was President, and carried out everything that I told him to do, and did it well.

Student: I once heard that you had said to one of your assistants that you would have liked to fire Hoover, but that you knew you couldn't get away with it with the Congress of the United States. Is this true?

President Truman: No, I didn't want to fire him. I gave

him a good calling down now and then, and it seemed to have the desired effect (*laughter and applause*).

Student: Mr. President, do you agree with the policy of not giving passports to men such as Paul Robeson who profess communism?

President Truman: If I were in the State Department and in charge of that, I'd be glad to give him a passport to get out of the country.

Student: How about travel to Red China? Do you think the State Department ought to allow it?

President Truman: If you want to take the risk, I don't see any reason why you shouldn't go over there, if you think you can get back (*laughter*).

Student: There are different kinds of hysteria, for instance, the hysteria of catching up, which we might be in now. I wonder if you think that there's any danger in the situation of continual stress of catching up with Russia?

President Truman: I think that the catching up is going to have to be on the other side of the fence, stretching everything they can to catch up, and the best thing for us to do is just to keep ahead of them.

Student: What I mean though, actually, is that a great deal of funds are now being allocated for scientific projects and scientific fellowships, and there's been some fear expressed by educators that the humanities and liberal arts will not be getting the attention that they should be getting.

President Truman: They should not be cast aside. I'm for the humanities and the liberal arts, and in addition to that, let's go ahead and do the other thing too. We can afford it. We've got the ability to do it.

Student: Mr. President, between the time that Senator McCarthy began his activities and the time that the Senate passed its censure resolution, well, a great deal of time elapsed. Do you feel that individual members of the Senate could have done more? Do you feel that any one of them could have spoken out? Do you feel that the fact that none of them did speak out is an indication of either the character of that particular Senate or of some feeling in our times?

President Truman: No, I don't take that attitude. I think some feeling in the times had something to do with that, but there were several Senators who hit McCarthy a lick, and that's how he got censured. Senator Flanders, I'm reminded, of Vermont up here, was early in the game; so was Senator Wayne Morse, and two or three others. They did the best they could, but you know to get things done in a majority-ruled government, you've got to have a majority, and it took a little while to get that majority convinced of what they ought to do. When they were convinced, they did it.

Student: Great protection against hysteria—mass hysteria against minorities especially—is, of course, the Bill of Rights. From the position you've taken on this, I imagine that you're for incorporating the first ten amendments into the due process clause of the Fourteenth. Now I was wondering do you include every single part in every one of those amendments in your . . .

President Truman: Those amendments are all a part of the law under which we live. You don't incorporate them into anything. They're there to be enforced, just the same as all the rest of the Constitution.

Student: There's a law in New York State, called the Sullivan Law, which prohibits the use of firearms or the carrying of them without a license, and this, it seems to me, violates one of the provisions of the Bill of Rights, which says that every citizen has the right to be safe in his home and can carry firearms.

President Truman: Well, in order to make him safe in his home, they had to arm the police, and that's his protection. There are so many users of those weapons of destruction privately, like the Al Capone gang and two or three others that I could name, that it was necessary to arm the police to prevent that sort of person carrying arms. I don't know whether you know it or not, but the bobbies in London don't carry any firearms. They just carry a club, and if they can't hit a fellow over the head with it and put him out of business, they don't shoot him right on the spot.

Student: This provision of the Bill of Rights provides that citizens, not policemen, may carry firearms. So, do you feel that the Sullivan Law is unconstitutional?

President Truman: Well, I don't know if it is or not, but it's a good thing (*laughter*).

Student: Mr. President, one of the biggest issues today, now, about rights is the integration problem. Could you tell us a little bit about the, well, the liberals' and conservatives' split which resulted in the Democratic Party because of this integration problem.

President Truman: I don't think there's any split in the Democratic Party on that issue. The split is in the Dixiecrat Party. I told you yesterday that with common sense and good will that situation can be worked out, because it's been

127

done in my home county and my home state. It can be done everywhere if it's approached by people of common sense and good will. That's all it takes. They cloud the issue with so many things that have no relation to it, which give some people a chance to hide behind something that they're not for. But in the long run, it has to be done; if we're going to be the leaders of the world, the Free World, and all the rest of the world eventually, we've got to perform at home just as we expect the people abroad to perform. For your information, I'm told that there are about 2,300,000,000 people in the world and about 800 or 900 million of them are white and the rest of them brown, red, and yellow. They have just as much right to the Bill of Rights as a man with a white skin, and that's what I'm for (*applause*).

Student: Well, right now the rules of the Senate provide the operating committees a great deal of latitude in their investigations. Now what changes would you recommend, if any, to prevent this sort of McCarthy type of thing that we've had?

President Truman: Good men in charge of those committees is the best remedy.

Student: How can you be assured of that?

President Truman: You've got to try them out and find out. If they're no good, then give them what's coming to them.

Student: Don't you think any procedural changes should be made?

President Truman: No. I don't think you can make any procedural change because the objective of a committee in the House or the Senate is to get the facts for legislation to cover something that ought to be legislated on. And you can't put a bridle on them. There isn't any reason to. But the chairman of the committee, if he believes in that Bill of Rights —and I'm speaking from experience—never allows those things to happen in a committee, any more than they would happen in a courtroom. But you have to have a man in charge who understands this thing and who is willing to enforce it. If he doesn't do it, there's nothing you can do about it but kick him out at the next election.

Student: How about the right of cross examination of a witness?

President Truman: Well, that's not necessary in a committee hearing. They have that right in the courts, and if a committee goes too far, and the fellow carries the thing to the courts, he gets everything that he ought to get. It's been done several times.

Student: You predicted that in our lifetime we will see another demagogue since there seem to be cycles of them, every thirty years or so, as you say. Do you think if our younger candidates continue to look like television announcers we'll recognize the demagogues when they come along *(laughter)*?

President Truman: I hope we will.

Student: I guess I should follow up on that *(laughter)*. I don't want to express my own personal opinion whether we will or not, but . . .

President Truman: You have a right to an opinion, same as I have.

Student: But do you think that the man with the very, very smooth delivery in the Senate and with the very, very fine-looking face, well, do you think the American people really know enough about politics from all of your travels and your speaking to them, to know that the man is selling them a bill of goods?

President Truman: I think they do. I think the American people are becoming better informed every day in the year. And I want to say to you, it's pretty hard to fool them, even when you've got something that's worth while to sell.

Student: Then how come there are so many Republicans in office?

President Truman: Because they had the most votes (*laughter*).

Student: Mr. President, assuming that another period of hysteria should come, what does an individual citizen who is not being directly persecuted, what should an individual citizen of that sort do?

President Truman: Well, he should analyze the situation and get on the side of right, just like they have in every instance of this kind.

Student: What specifically should he do, I mean, a person with no political power whatsoever?

President Truman: Well, I don't know what's going to happen. He should inform himself. The best way in the world is to inform himself. We've got the best means of information that there is, because in addition to the newspapers you've got radio and television.

Student: Mr. President, all through history there's been a utilization of the "big lie," I guess, in politics, and I was just wondering, do you think that this big lie, which is being utilized today over television, radio, is to a far greater degree than ever before? Has it created or at least contributed to the hysteria?

President Truman: Yes. There isn't any doubt about that. It's too bad that that can happen. It has happened in the case of Hitler and Mussolini. It's happened in the case of McCarthy and two or three others of our famous demagogues, but there's very little that you can do about it unless you can prove, publicly, without the danger of a slander suit, that they are guilty of telling what isn't so.

Student: Mr. President, what does a citizen do when it's not the public that gets hysterical, but the government? That is, what is a citizen to do when his government makes pacts with countries that are completely opposed to everything that our Constitution stands for, because a part of the government feels that this is important for our security? I mean, I'm speaking specifically about Spain.

President Truman: Yes, it's Spain that you're talking about, and I know what you're talking about. I was against it one hundred percent, but I'll tell you this, that the only way you can remedy that is to be sure that the man who makes the treaties with the world and is responsible for foreign policy believes that he's doing what's right. Of course, you always have a chance to get at him every four years.

Student: Another manifestation of hysteria, rather a symptom, is lynching. In Samuel Lubell's book, *The Future of American Politics*, he accuses you of being against an antilynching bill, but that you would not vote against it because you had a great many Negro constituents. Is this true?

President Truman: I wonder if he ever read the record. I was against lynching every time it came up, maybe half a dozen times. I mean I voted for the antilynching bill.

Student: You said you had to?

President Truman: No. I didn't say anything of the kind, because I never had to do anything when I was in the Congress. I voted for what I thought was right. And I voted for the antilynching bill. I don't want to see anybody lynched, no matter what he's done. He ought to have a trial, and if they want to hang him, they can do it (*laughter and applause*).

Professor Rogers: Years ago, when I was the age of these panelists, at the Johns Hopkins University, there was a lectureship known as the Turnbull Lectures on Poetry. The president of Johns Hopkins in those days was an amiable chemist who usually, when he opened his mouth, put his foot in it. He once introduced as a Turnbull lecturer a gentleman who was to be my future colleague and dear friend at Columbia, but before he did so, he read off the list of previous lecturers: Brunetière from France, someone from Germany, Childs and Kittredge from Harvard, and Edmund Gosse from England. Turning to the lecturer of the day, he said: "It's a very distinguished list. I'm sure we shall not be able to keep up the standard we have set for ourselves (*laughter*); our lecturer for today is Professor A. V. Williams Jackson of Columbia University, a great authority on Persian poetry."

Well, now, in respect to this Radner Foundation, we certainly won't be able to keep to the standard that we have set for ourselves in this first series. It was my good fortune to persuade President Truman, on behalf of the Department of

132

Public Law and Government, to consent to deliver these lectures. The character of the lectures was of his choosing, that is, a few minutes of talk by himself and then questions from the panelists. And he insisted that his audience be composed in considerable part of Columbia College students and Barnard College students. I'm going to ask Dean Palfrey if, on behalf of Columbia College, he won't add to the gratitude that I've expressed on behalf of the Department of Public Law and Government (*applause*).

Dean Palfrey: On behalf of all of us at Columbia, Mr. President, these last three days we won't forget. You're a great teacher, as well as a great man, and all we can say, and I think quickly, is thanks (*applause*).